The Artful

Mandala

COLORING BOOK

The Artful Mandala

COLORING BOOK

....

Creative Designs
for Fun and Meditation

....

CHER KAUFMANN

THE COUNTRYMAN PRESS · WOODSTOCK, VT.

The Countryman Press
Woodstock, Vermont
www.countrymanpress.com

A division of W. W. Norton & Company, Inc.,
500 Fifth Avenue, New York, NY 10110
www.wwnorton.com

For information about special discounts for bulk purchases, please contact W. W. Norton Special Sales at specialsales@wwnorton.com or 800-233-4830.

Printed in The United States

The Artful Mandala Coloring Book
978-1-58157-352-7 (pbk.)

10 9 8 7 6 5 4 3 2

Contributors:

Maria Tullos, pg 17, 119
Jane Cole, pg 21
Sue-Ellen Hegel, pg 23, 123
Judy McIntosh, pg 37, 197
Stacy Swierenga, pg 41, 71
Solina Maquis, pg 57, 147
Georgia Browne, pg 59
Margaret Correa, pg 93
Jane Prouty, pg 103, 127
Barbara R. Sadler, pg 113
Tracy Vega, pg 117, 199

"Every child is an artist.
The problem is how to remain an artist once he grows up."

—PABLO PICASSO

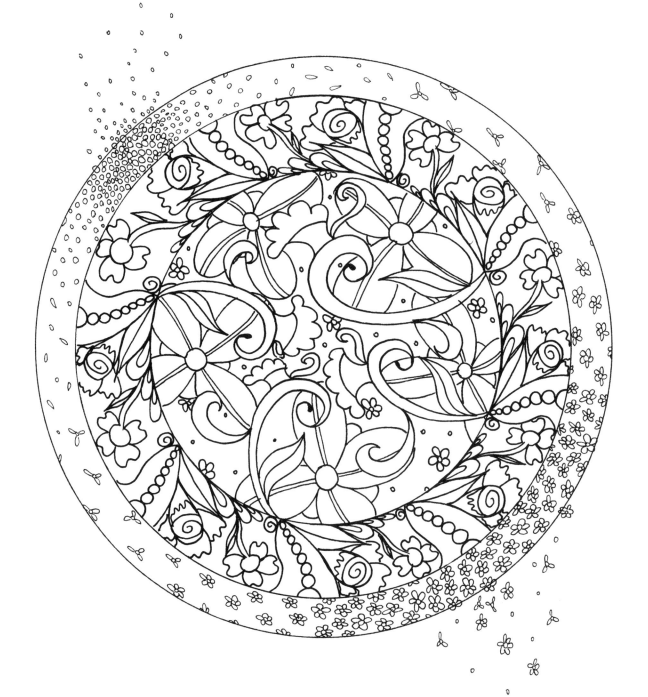

Welcome to the magical world of *The Artful Mandala Coloring Book: Creative Designs for Fun and Meditation.*

Coloring brings the artist out in everyone, regardless of age. There is freedom in gathering colored pencils, markers, and crayons, laying them out, and feeling the anticipation of awe as the unfolding from colorless to colorful begins. For those who have always enjoyed drawing and coloring, *The Artful Mandala Coloring Book* creates little escapes from your regular world into pattern play you are familiar with and can easily connect to. For those who are new to coloring, there is no right or wrong way to approach it; there is only coloring. That's it!

Our brains love to work with and recognize patterns. When we color patterns, our minds can relax into the designs and our bodies and thoughts can drift into a calm place with each stroke of the color. Our whole beings benefit from a little time out from the hustle and bustle of the day and a little connection with our creative side. Pablo Picasso is quoted as saying "Every child is an artist. The problem is how to remain an artist once he grows up." Here, in *The Artful Mandala Coloring Book*, both child and adult are artists.

When I was a child, drawing and coloring were just for fun. But by the time I was in college, art for me expanded to include screen printing, photography, etching, monoprinting, woodblock printing, and more—not only as a study but also as expression. I was always interested in how patterns and lines moved and, depending on the light or the combination, the result could vary greatly. I won first place in a photography contest for a photograph that was about pattern observation. Over time, I studied patterns by looking at nature's arrangements and relationships, plus faces, behavior, and emotional energy patterns. I have licensure and a private practice for massage therapy, plus extensive studies in Energy Healing Arts including teaching Reiki and other energy awareness classes for many years. I am Chinese Face Reader, photographer, Inspirational Artist and teacher. I have learned that shapes, lines, and forms, seen and unseen, in every culture have importance by design. My experience has shown that our culture needs a little bit of creativity support.

Each of the mandala coloring designs are hand drawn; each pattern is created uniquely to that particular page and especially for you to color. There are no computer-generated images, and the process of drawing them is just as enjoyable as it will be for you to color them, with all the special points listed below in consideration. These pages are designed to be fun, relaxing, meditative, and a place where the mind can relax and play.

Suggestions on how best to delight in your coloring experience:

HAVE FUN! First and last is always enjoyment! This is your time to play, enjoy it!

RELAX. There is nothing here but you, the designs, and the colors. Breathe, both in and out, drop your shoulders down, relax your mouth, and relax your thoughts. Solutions come from interesting places when we let them surface.

EXPLORE! After playing with the colors on a few pages, explore using them differently to see what kind of result they can produce. If you normally use reds to color flowers for instance, try using blues. Colors have an effect on our emotions and behaviors. Cooler, calmer colors tend to be the blues, greens, and purples. Warmer, more stimulating colors such as reds, oranges, and yellows tend to create a feeling of vibrancy. If you have a gold or silver pencil/pen, adding little touches that reflect light can be amazing!

DELICIOUS! The Yummy Sounds. This is an important one! When you eat something delicious, do you notice how you often say "oooo!" or "mmmm!" or "Oohhhh!"? The same response shows up when you are amazed. While you are exploring *The Artful Mandala Coloring Book*, notice when you color something and you hear yourself or someone else make a yummy sound. Be amazed. "Oooo!"

LA LA LA. If you are a person who loves music, you might discover coloring can be influenced by the music you play in the background. If you like to work with silence as your music, that counts, too! If you have other kinds of sounds around you, you might find that as you get into your coloring the sounds disappear into the background and the peace of the coloring begins to be bigger than the sounds.

HAVE FUN! First and last is always enjoyment! Drop into the ocean of color you create with each page. Swim in blues and swirl in pinks, bloom in oranges, grow in greens, and bring enthusiasm with reds.

Curious about colors? Colors mean different things to different people and to different cultures. Color can represent emotions or specific items (green=plants, blue=water). There are cultures and studies that discuss connections of colors to specific organs of the body, frequencies of light (rainbows show this), and how nature uses color to create attraction or caution signals. In fact, color is such an integral part of our everyday life, in-depth studies have shown which colors are used to influence us in marketing decisions (what we buy or where we eat and how long we stay!). But color is also used to create a feeling of a room and can sometimes determine which clothes we wear on that special day. In *The Artful Mandala Coloring Book*, there are no rules as to which colors you use or where you use them. Here you are the creative artist able to use colors to explore and express. For the inquisitive artist, here is a brief list of what colors can represent.

PURPLE - imagination, royalty and regality, coolness, creativity, intellect, magic, intuition

BLUE - calmness, coolness, serenity, depth, communication (think of water as a conduit), wisdom, loyalty

GREEN - growth, spring, newness, freshness, coolness, harmony, balance, internal strength

YELLOW - courage, willpower, warmth, intellect, joy, encouragement, connection

ORANGE - creating new things, things in motion, warmth, strength, endurance, optimism

RED - vibrancy, heat, passion, love, power, danger, intensity, determination

BLACK - mystery, undiscovered places, hidden places, unknown, power, elegance

WHITE - peace, clarity, purity, cleanliness, perfection

GOLD - wealth, elegance, abundance, success

SILVER - cool, wealth, intellect, feminine, mystery

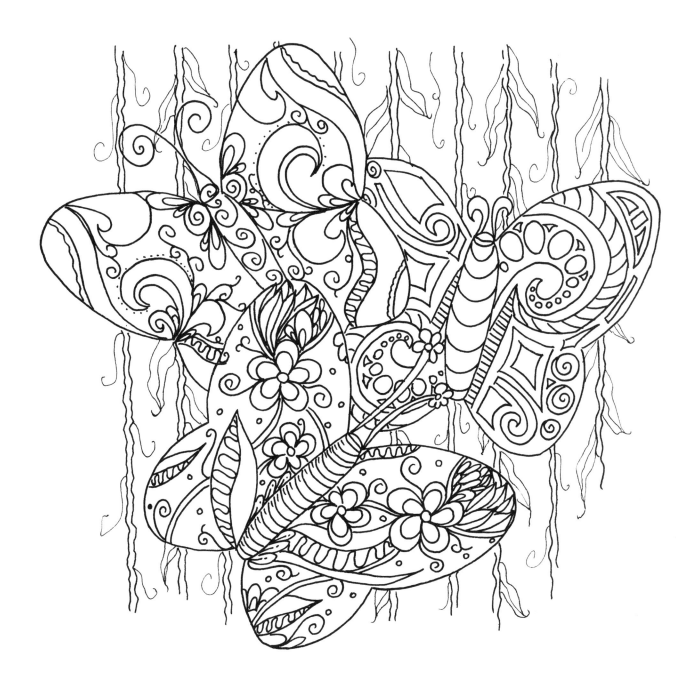

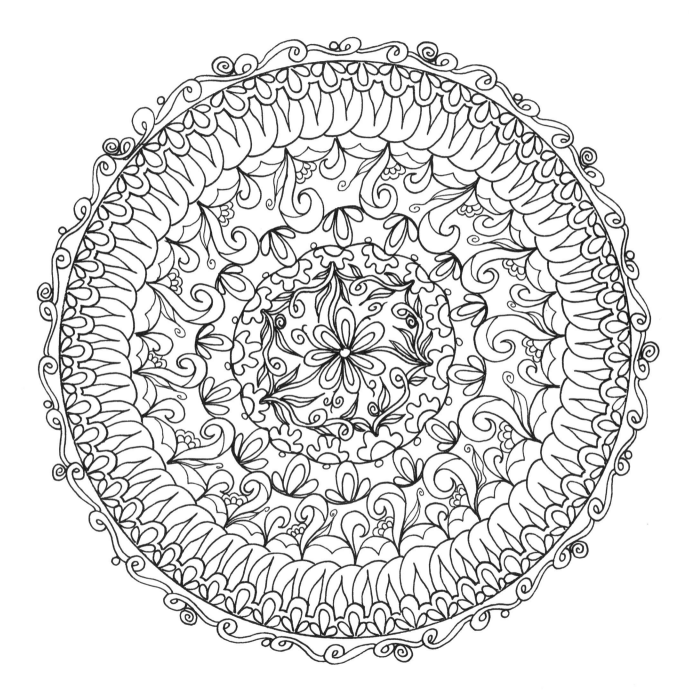

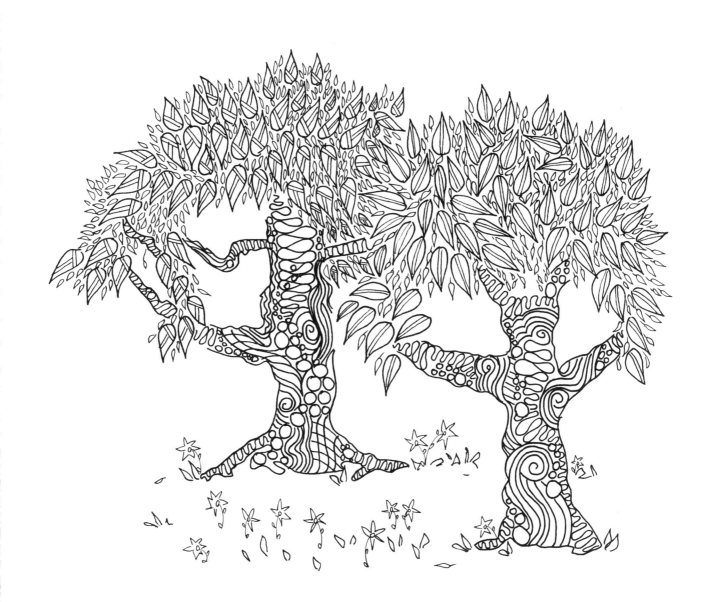

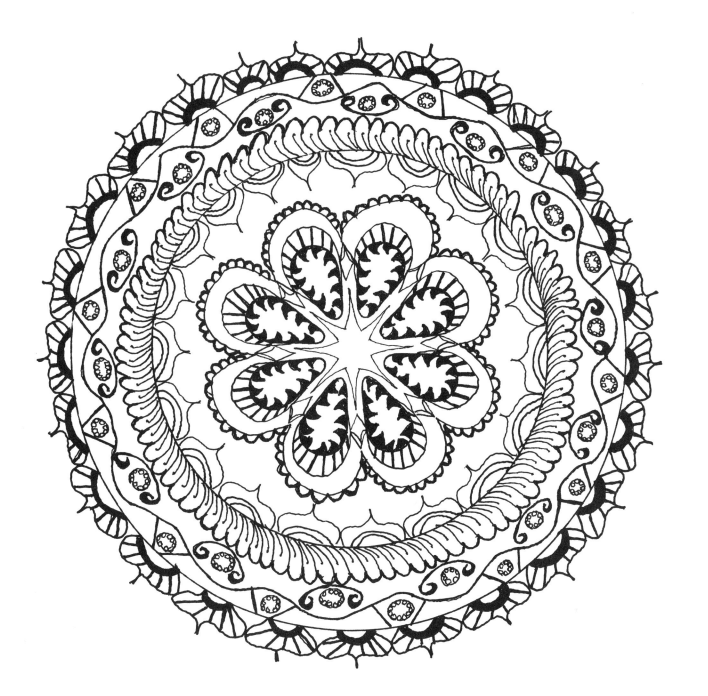

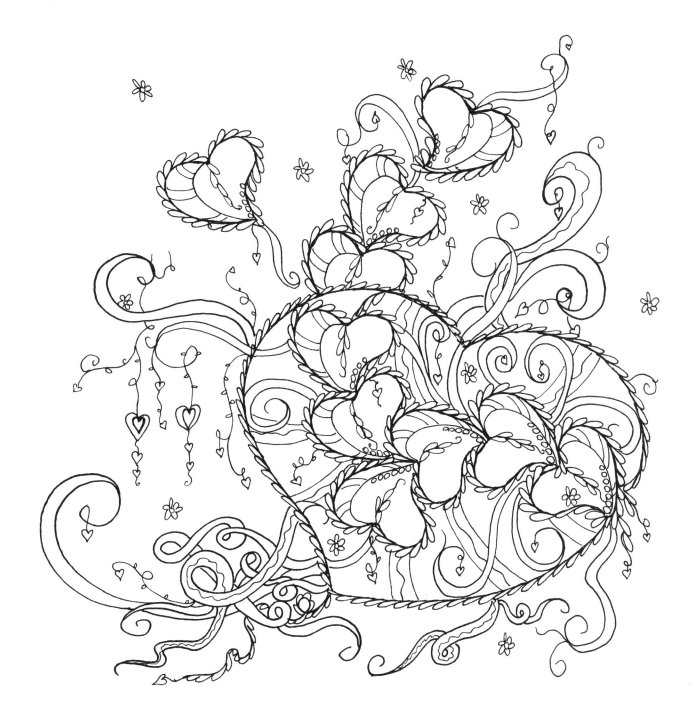

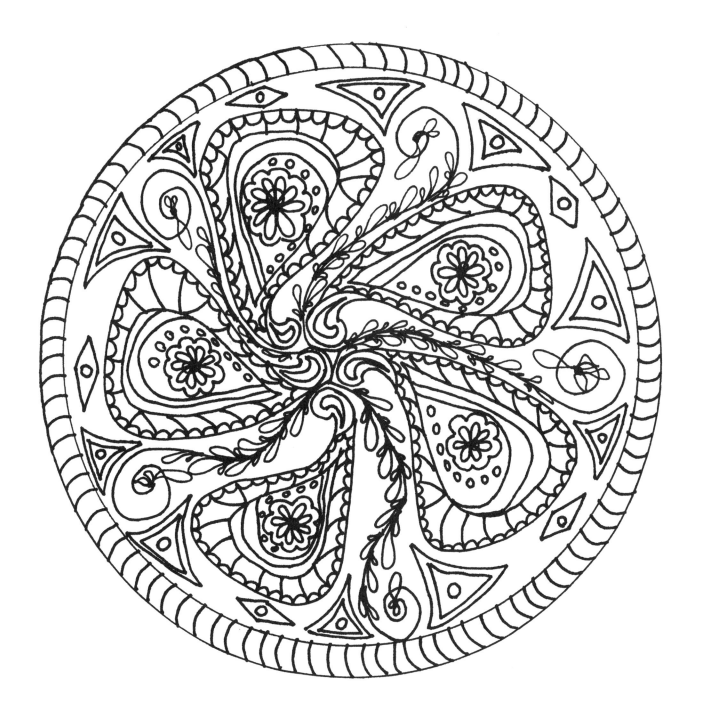

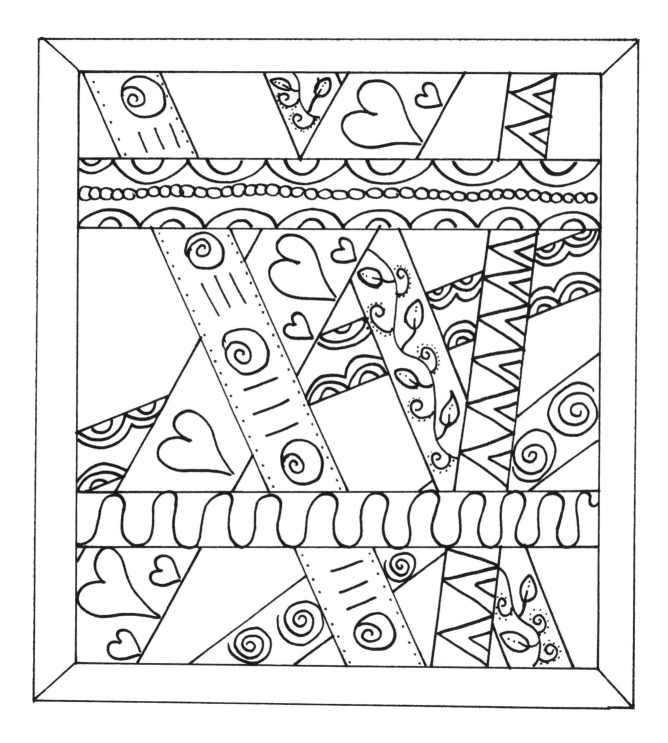

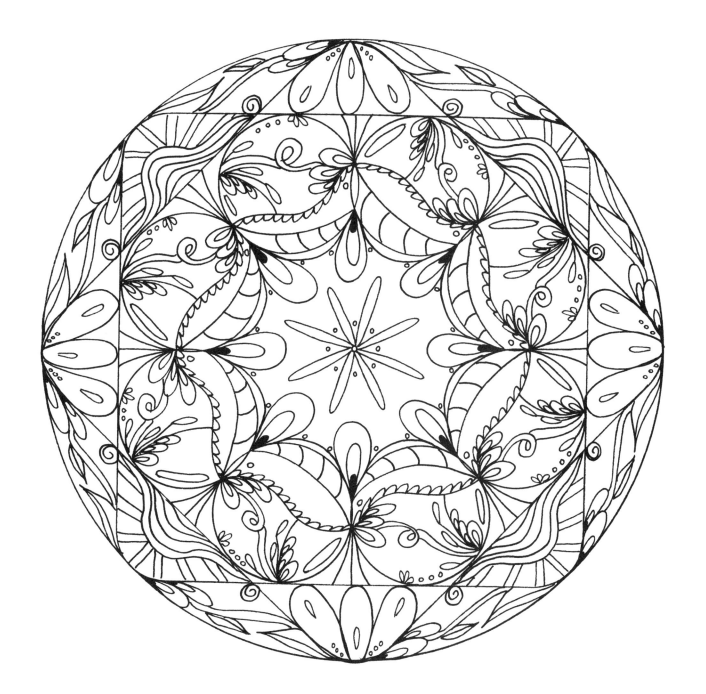

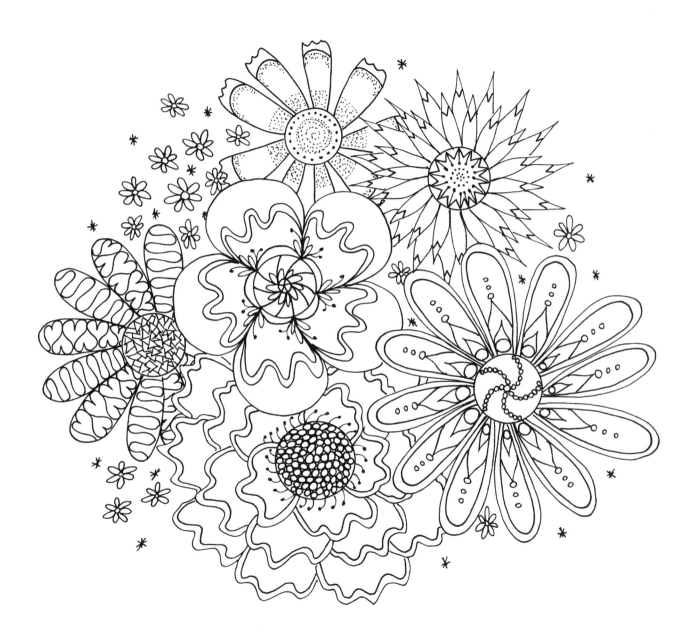

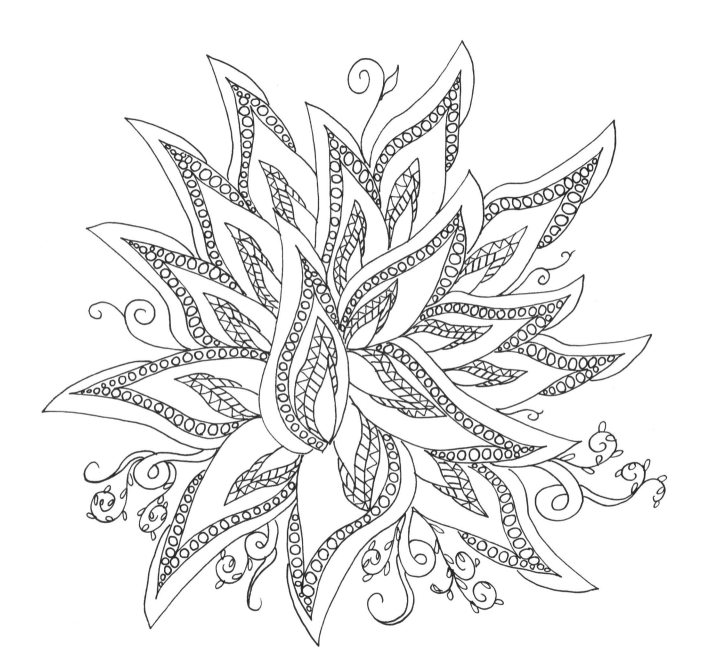

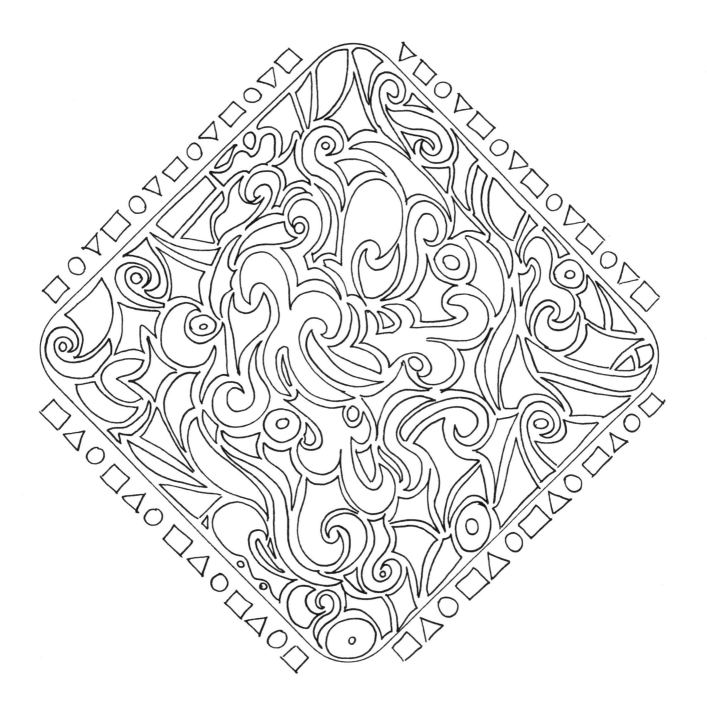

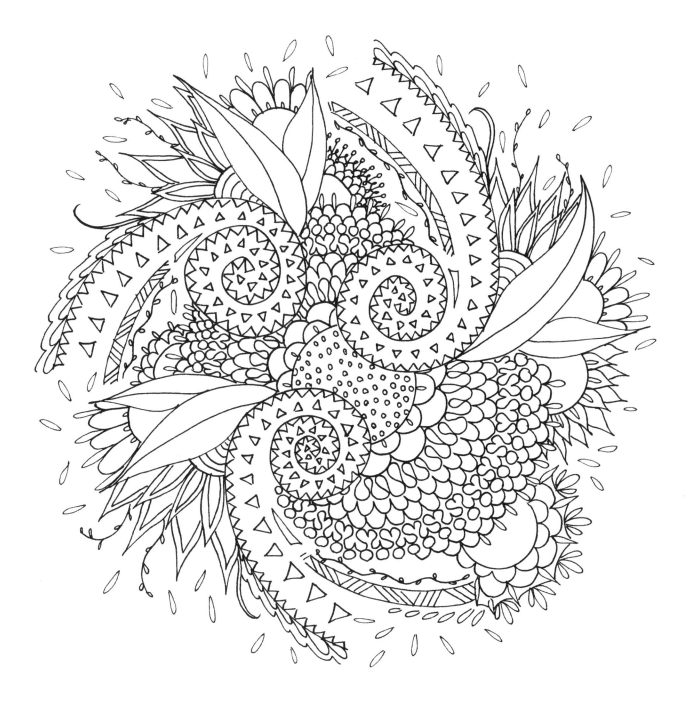

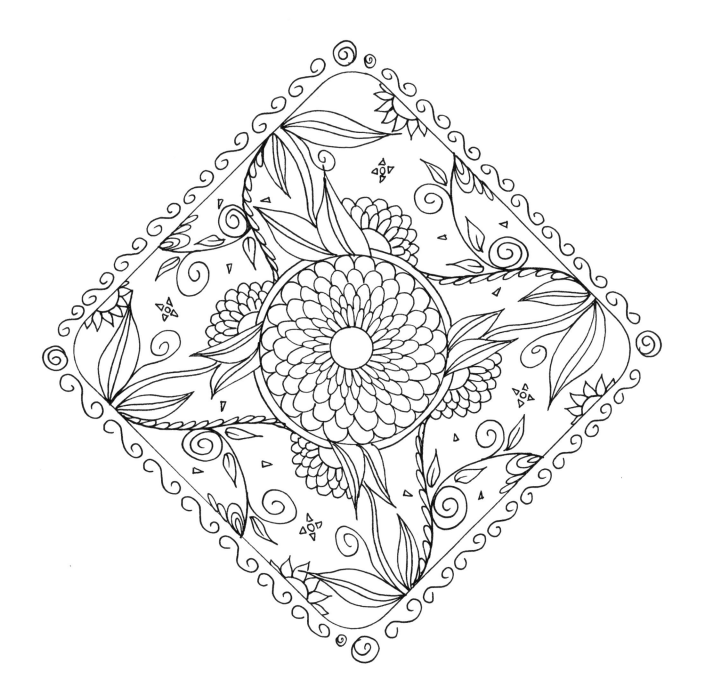

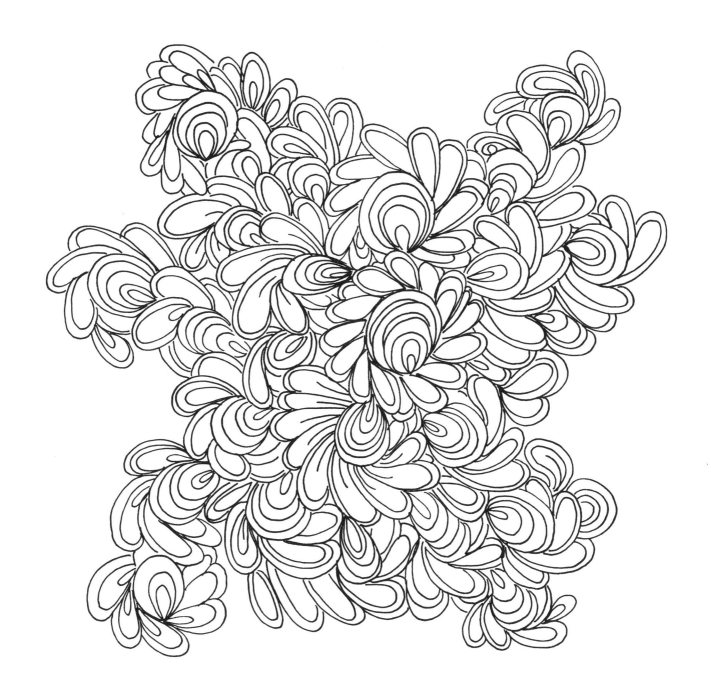

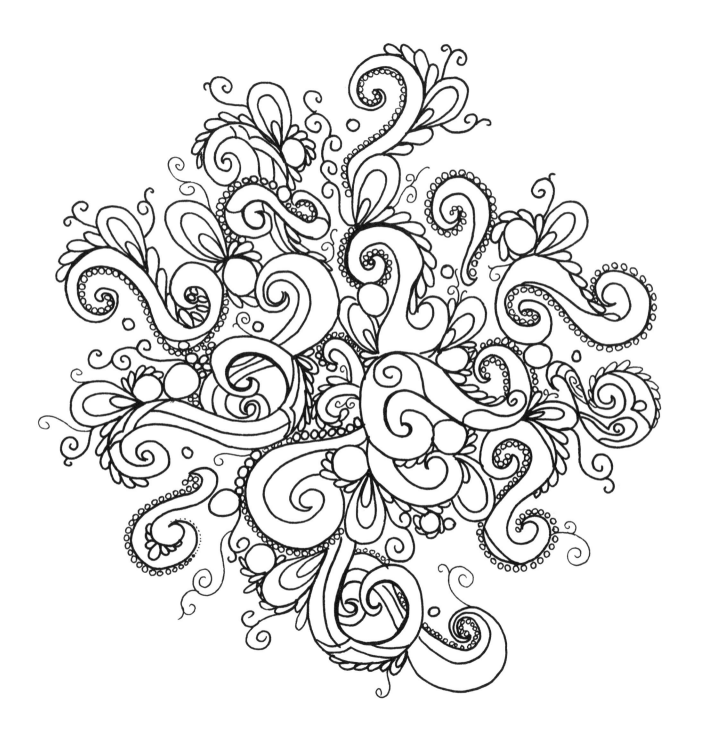

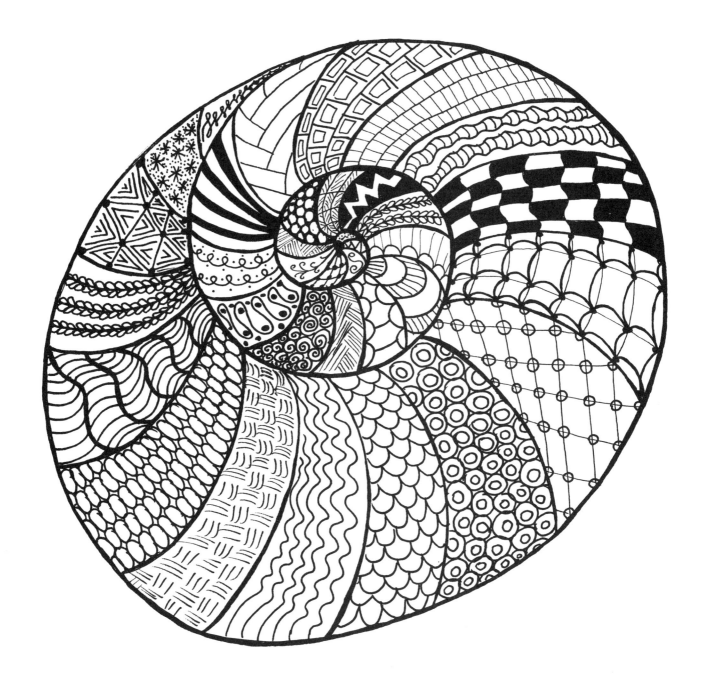

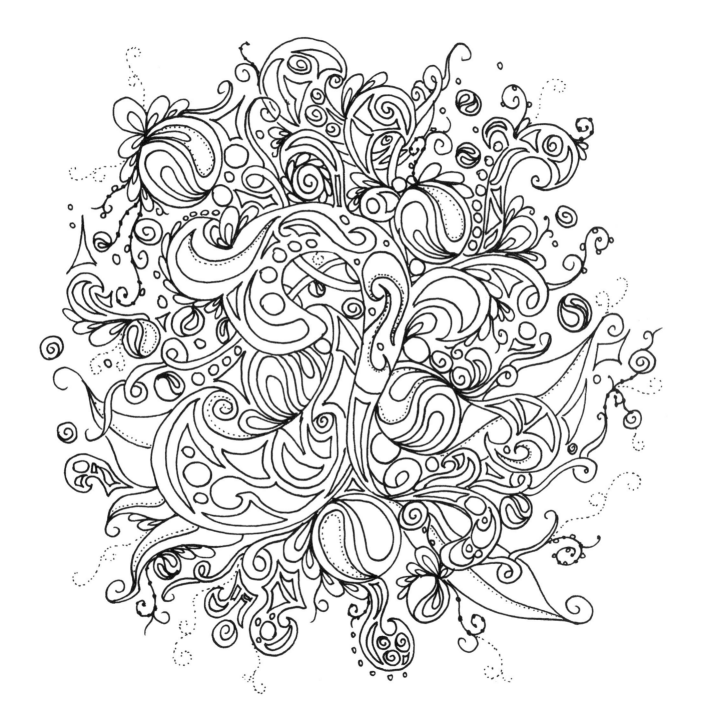

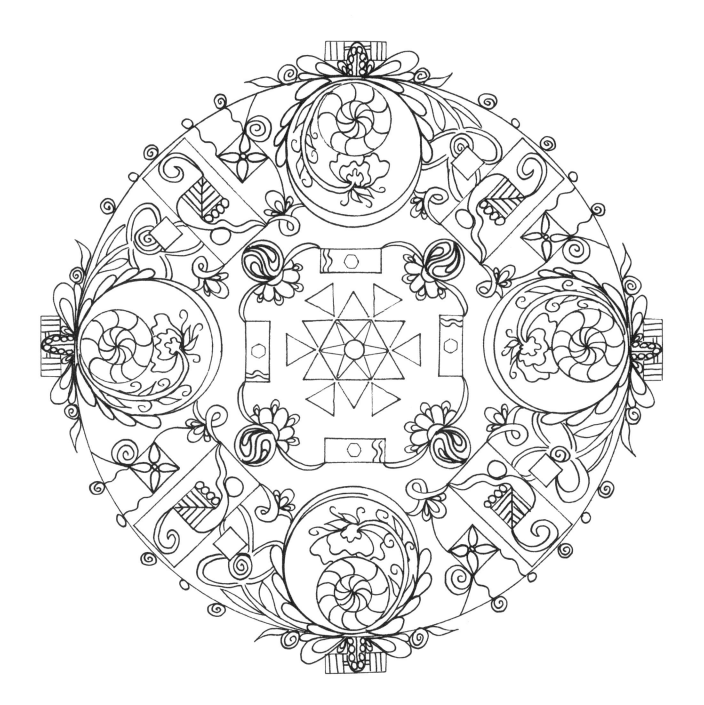

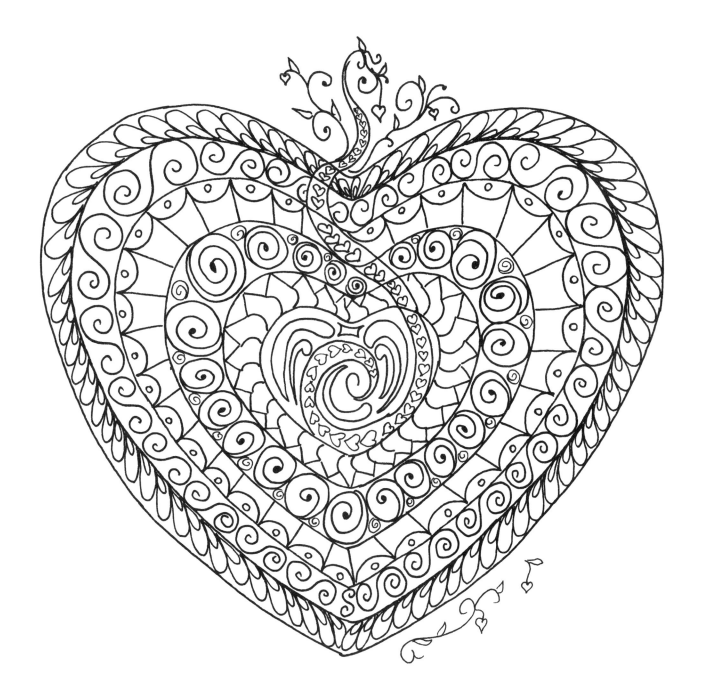

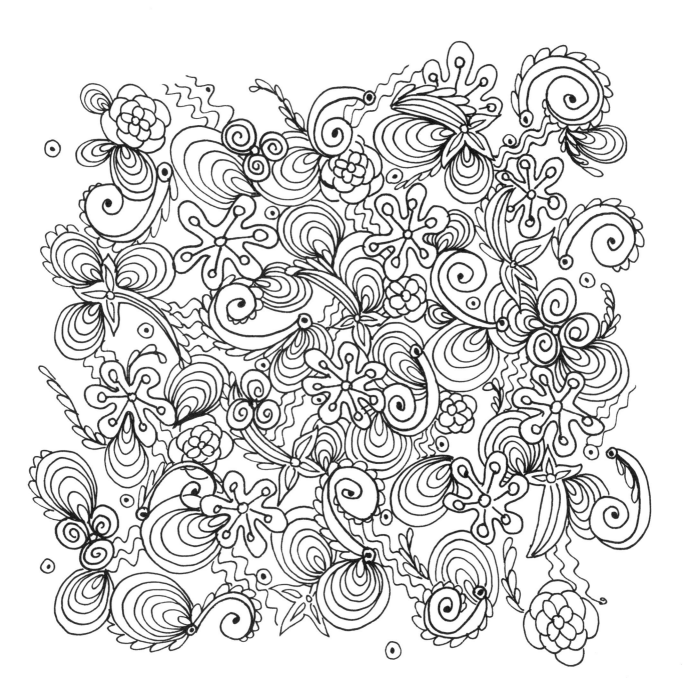

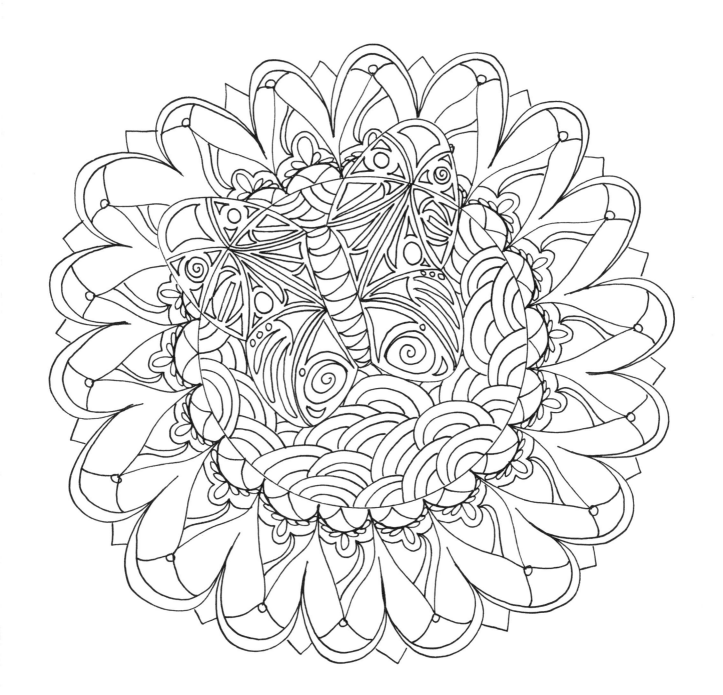

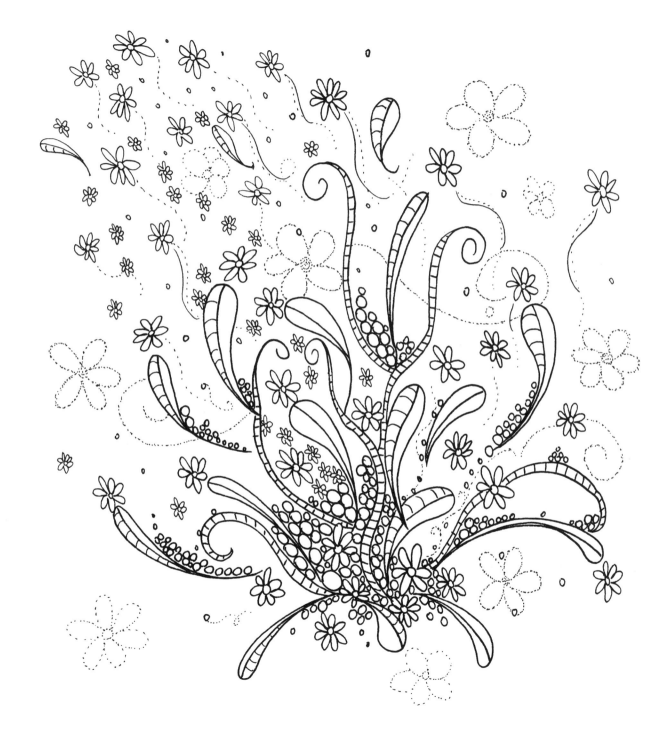

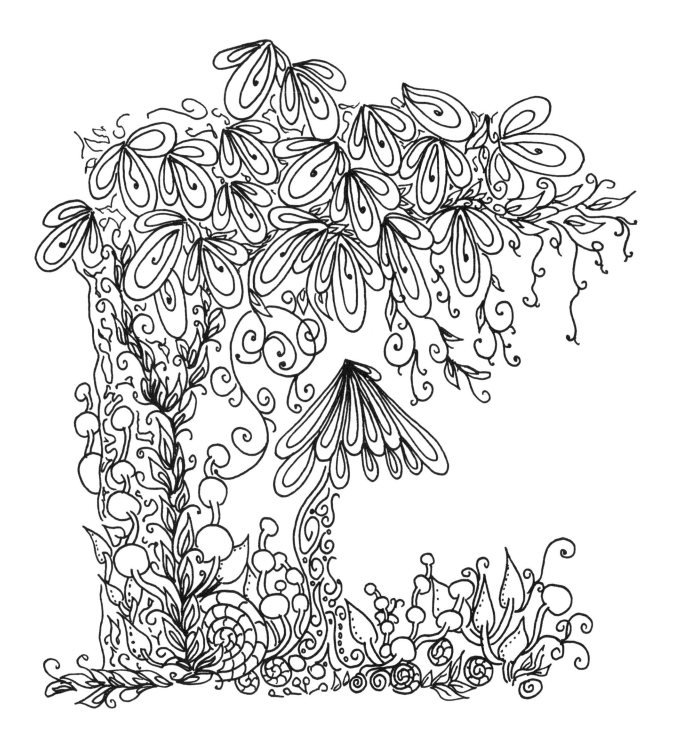

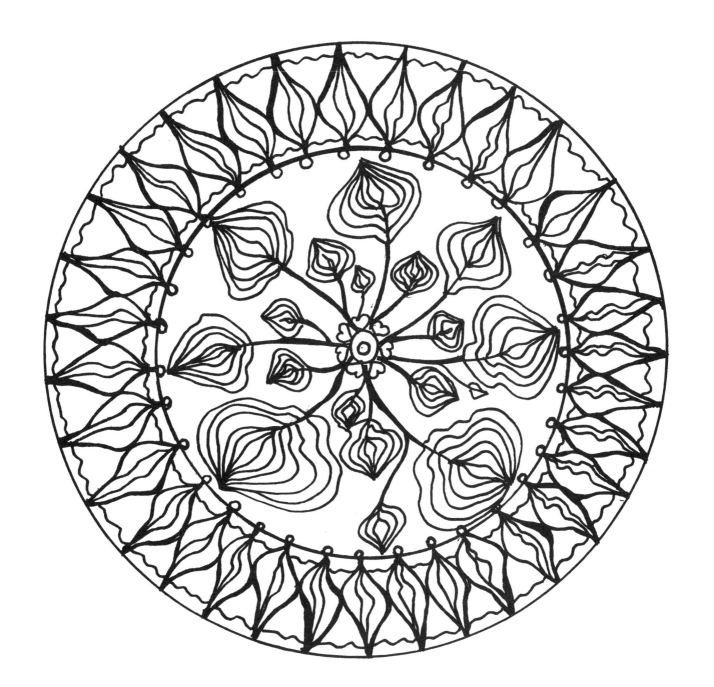

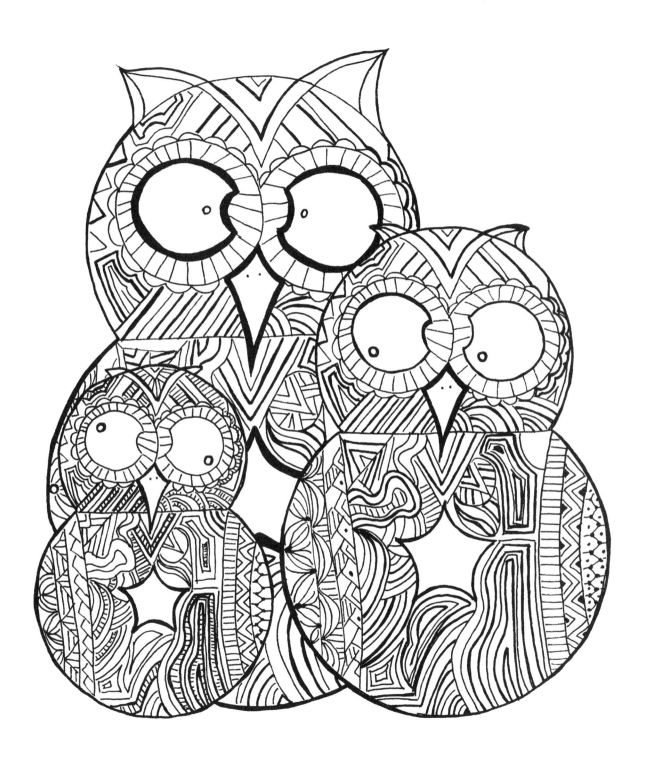

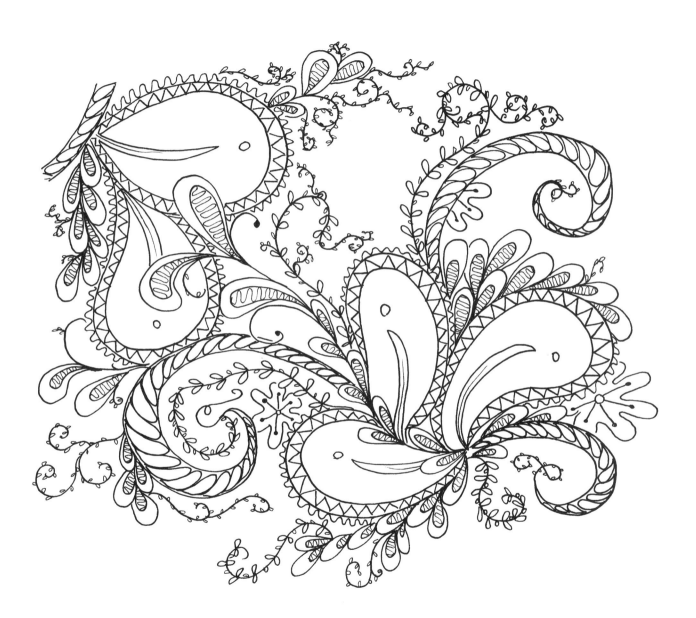

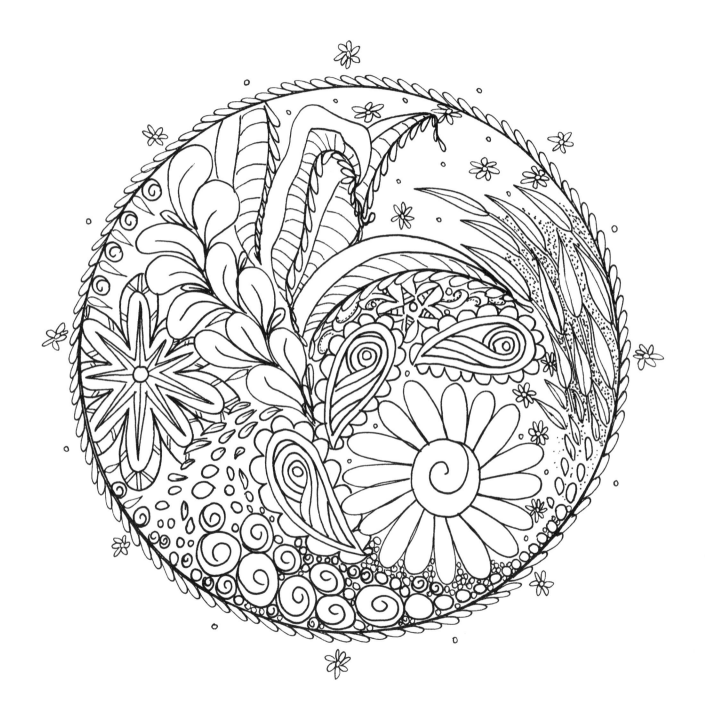

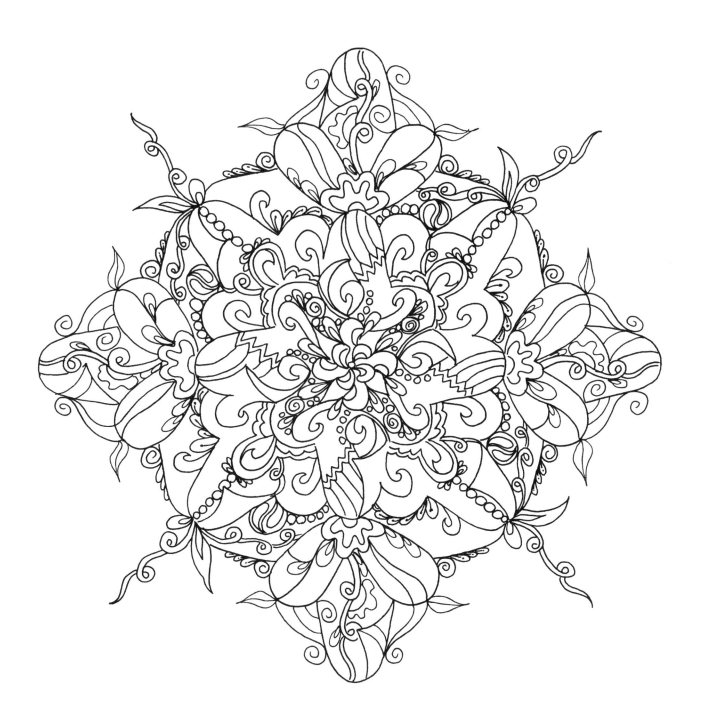

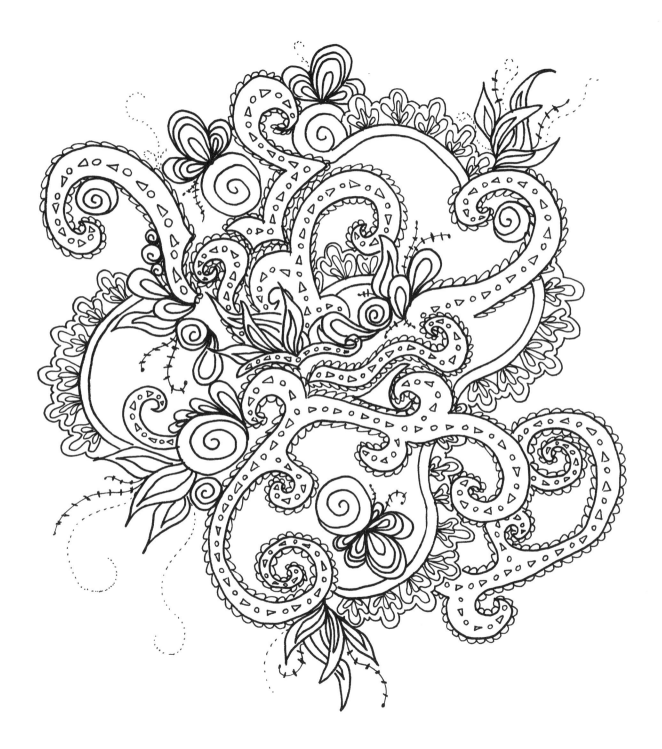

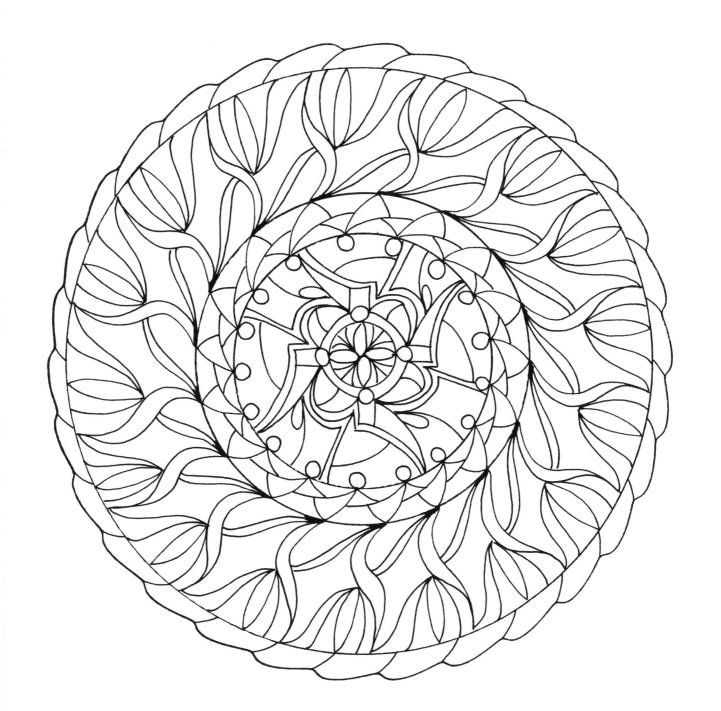

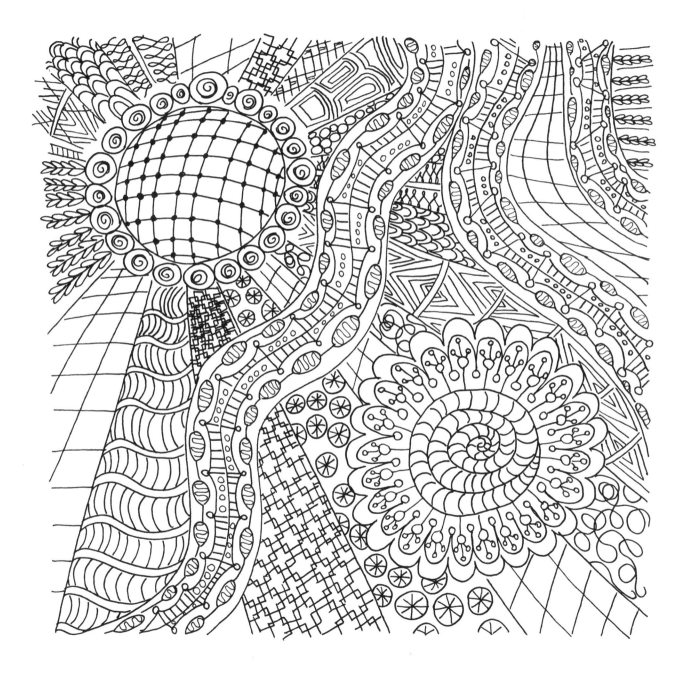

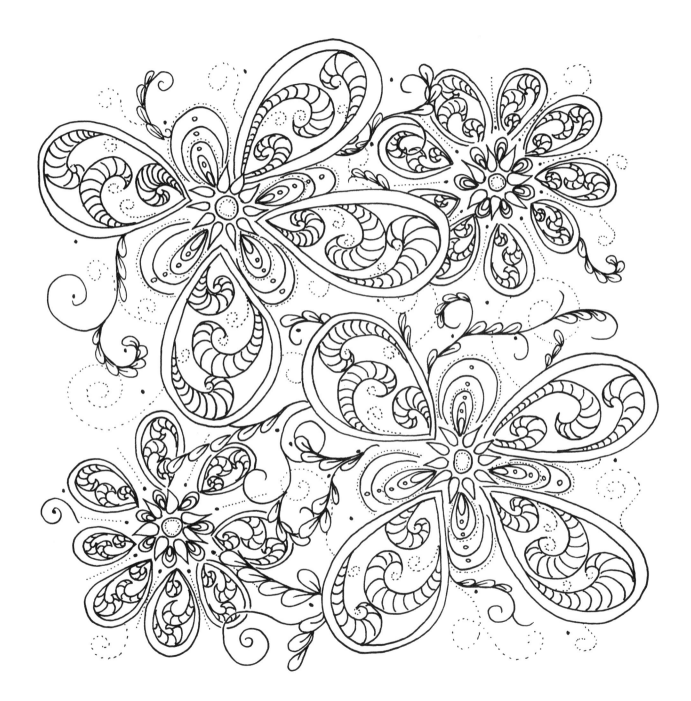

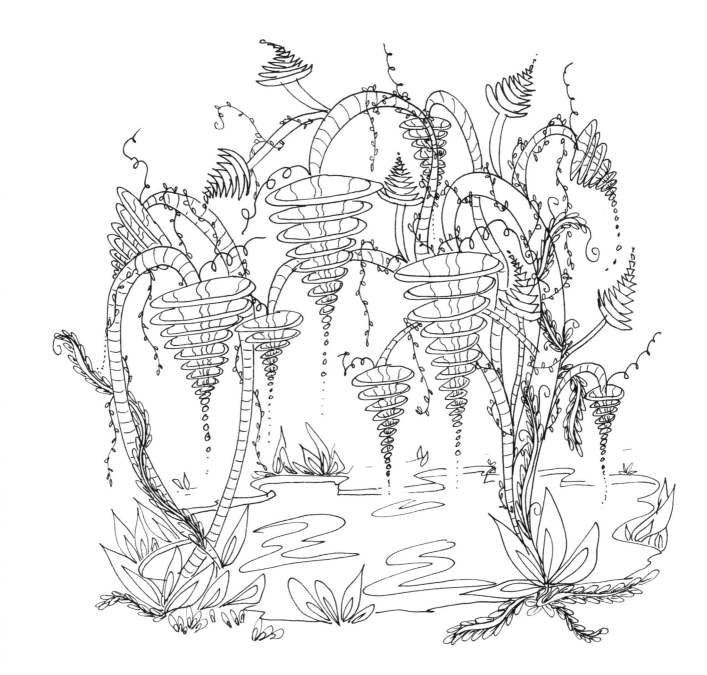

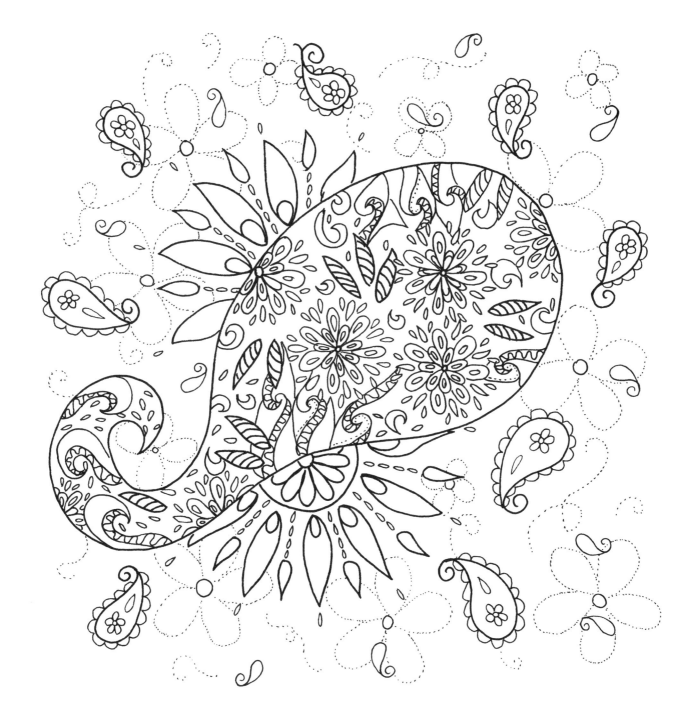

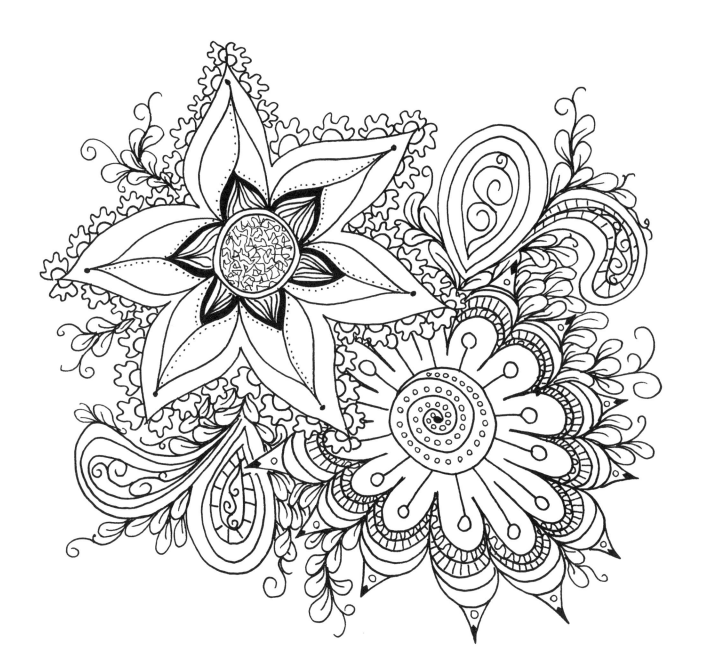

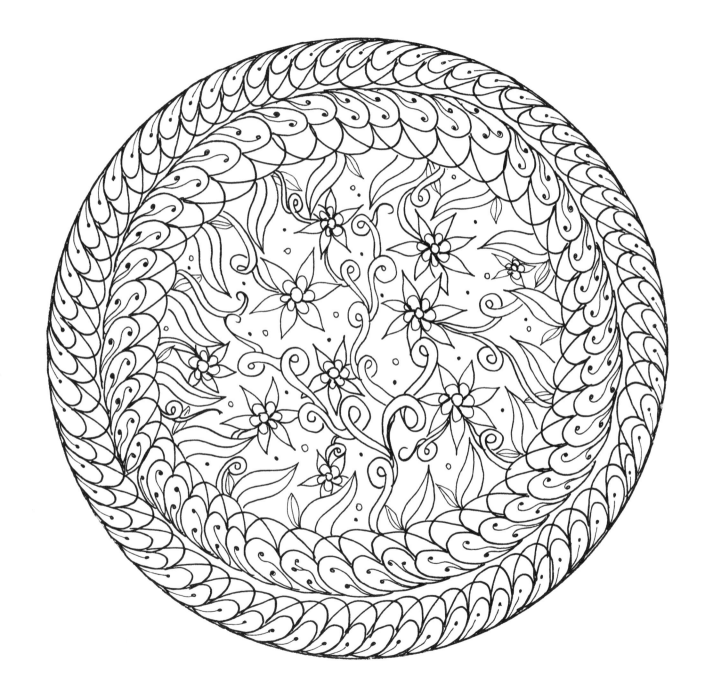

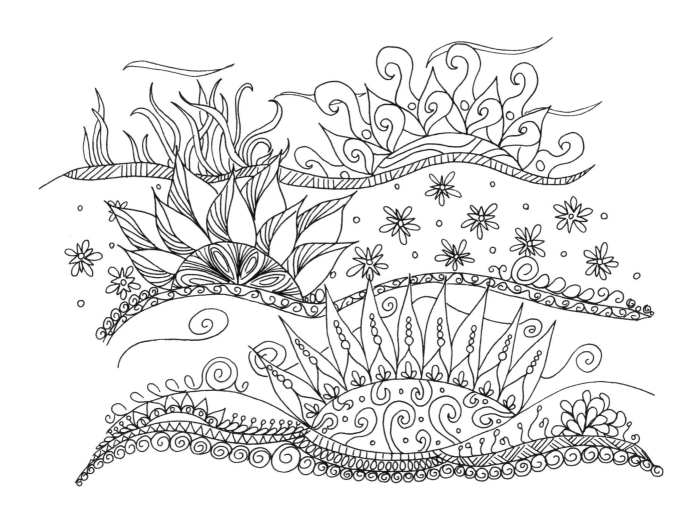

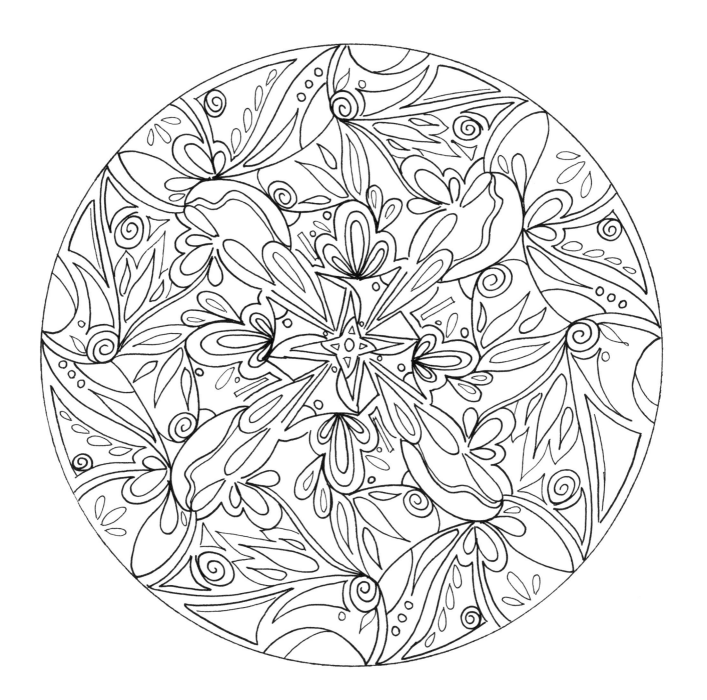

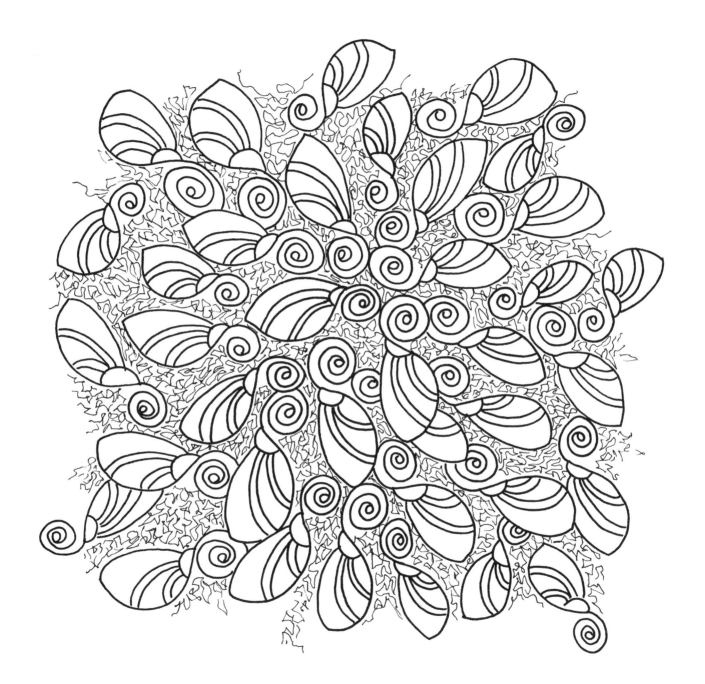

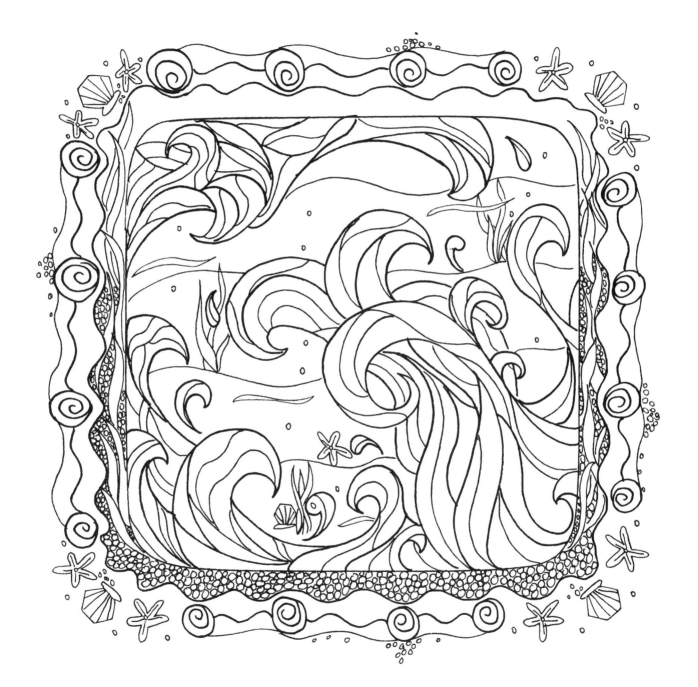

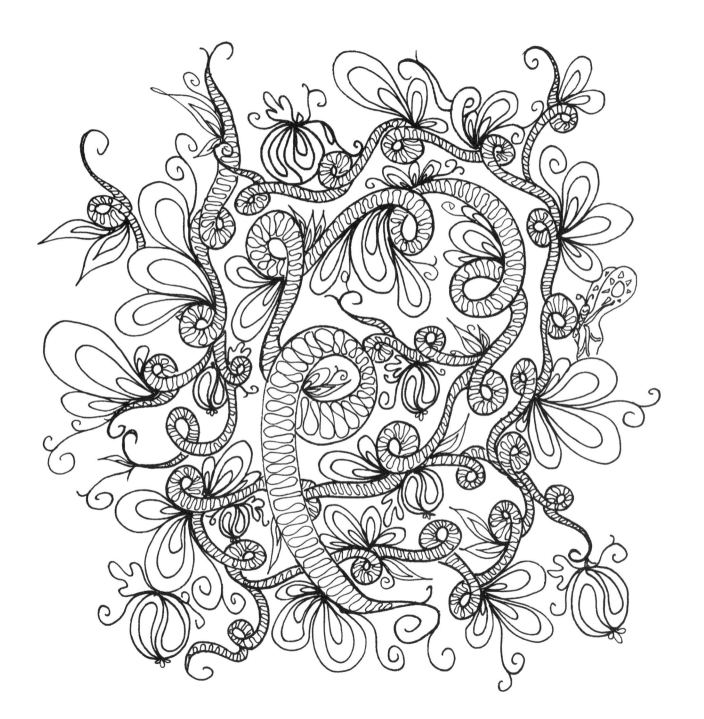

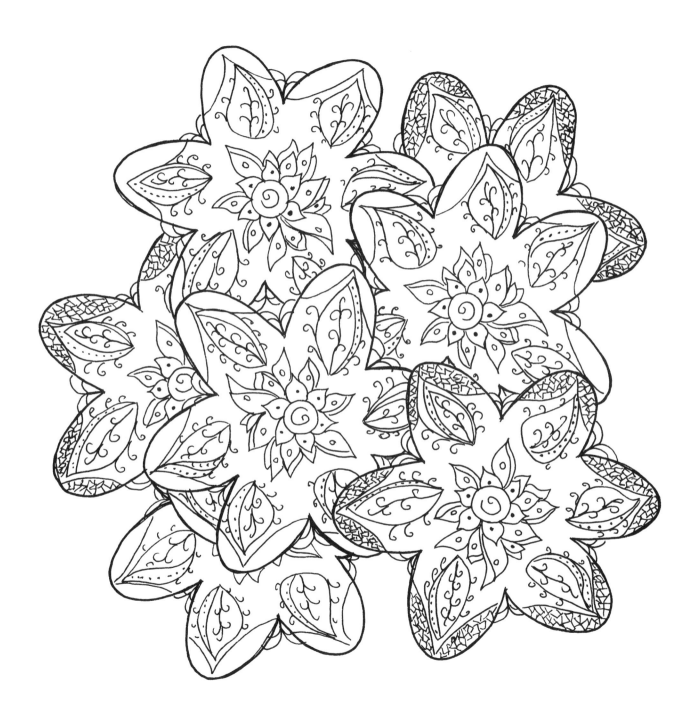

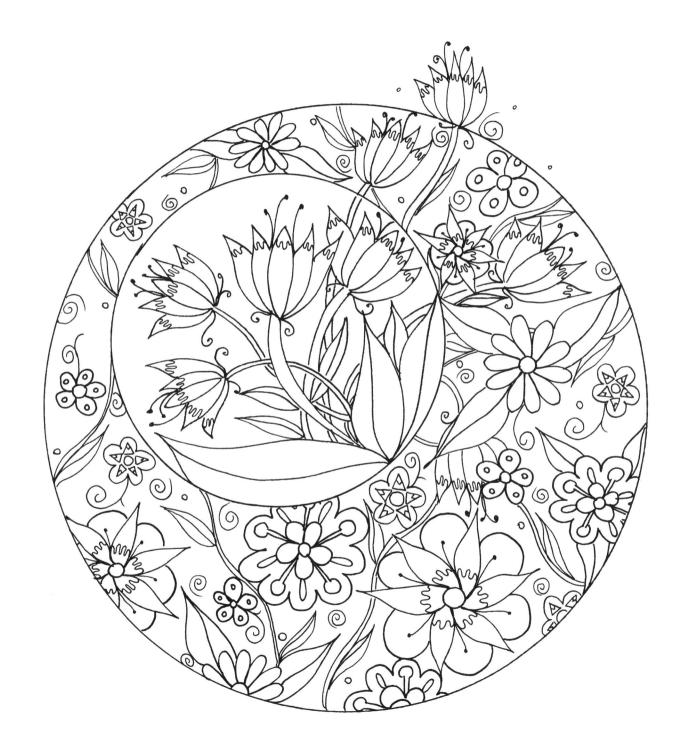

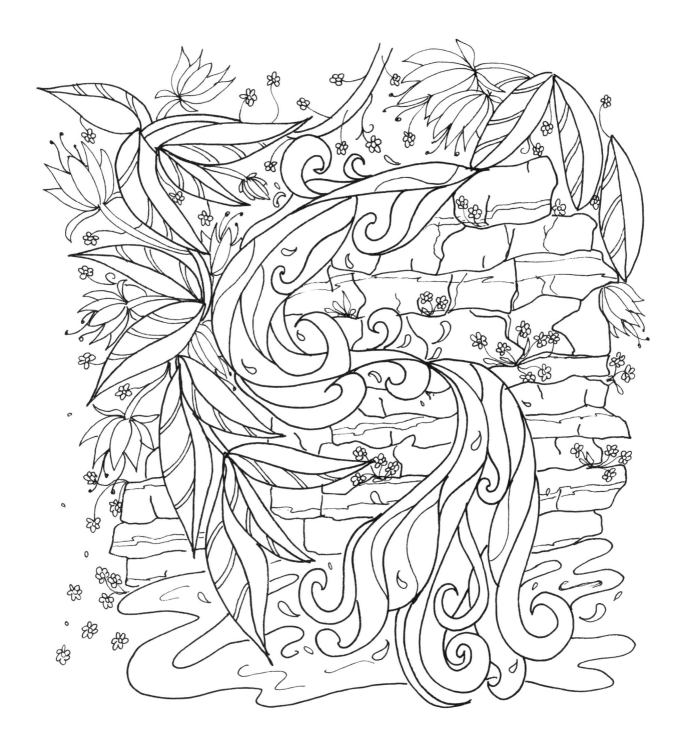

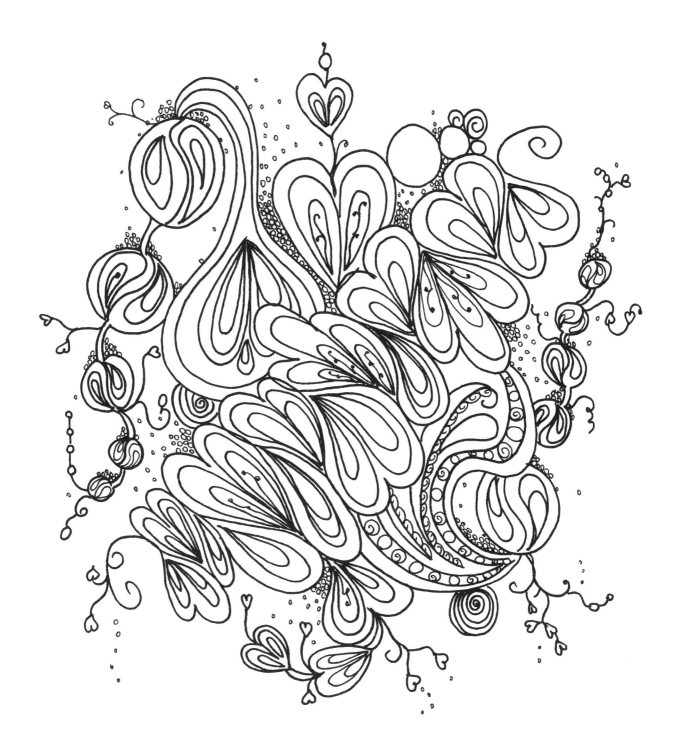

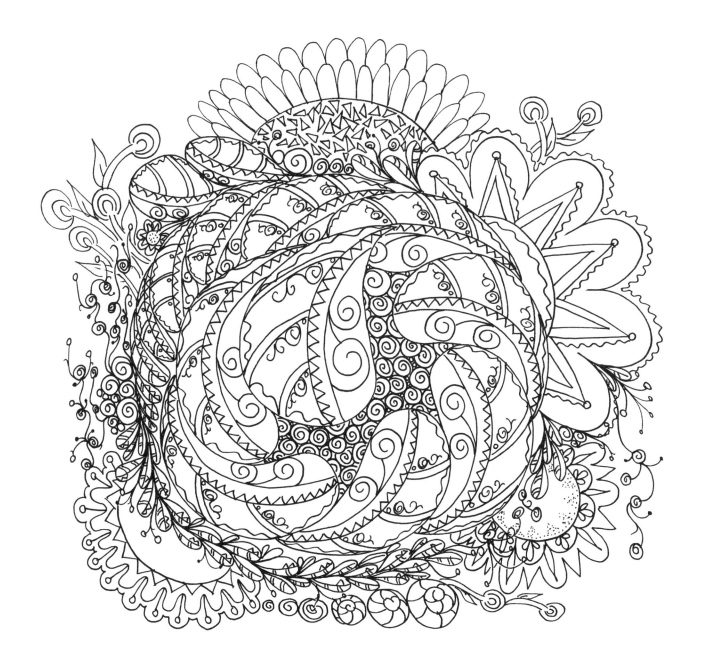

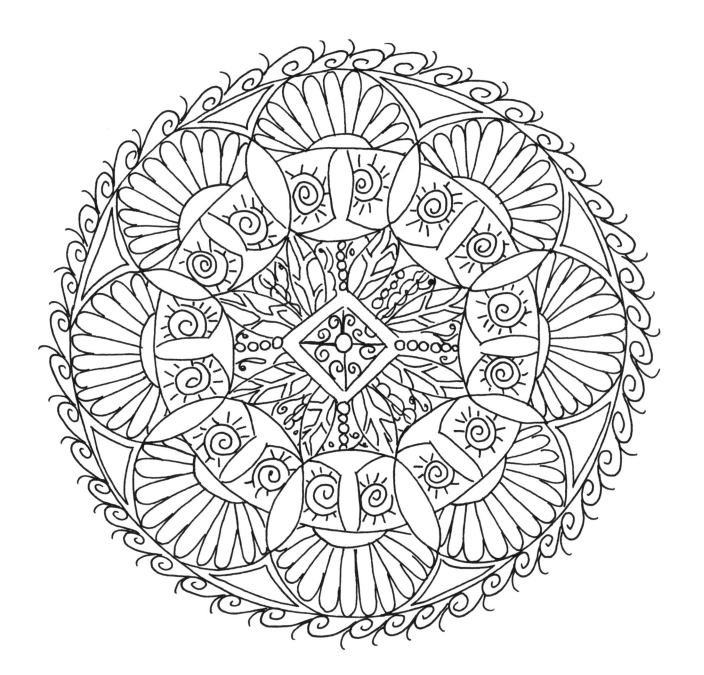

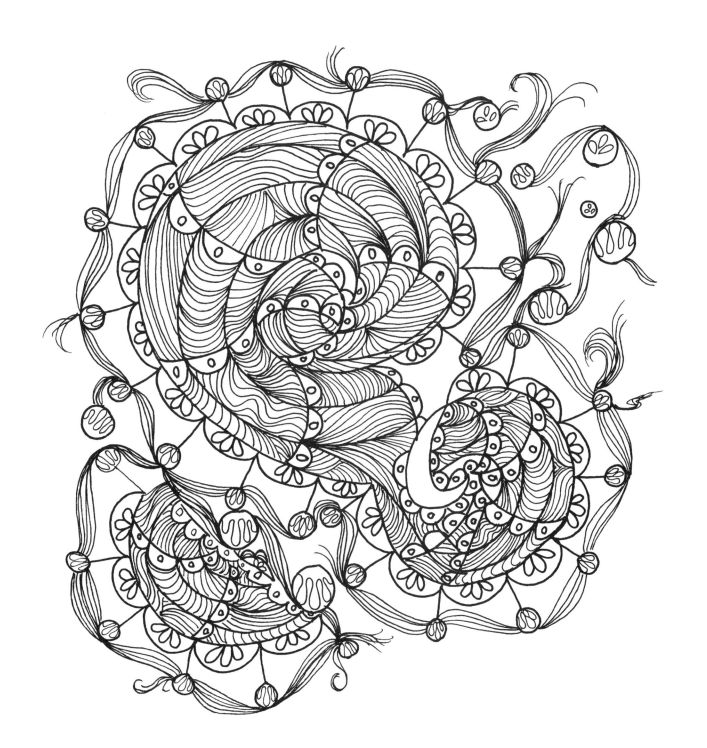

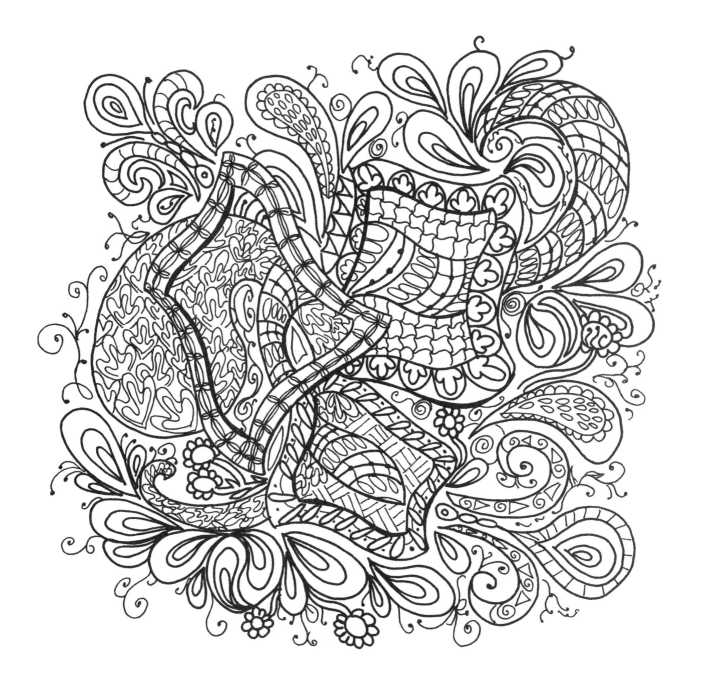

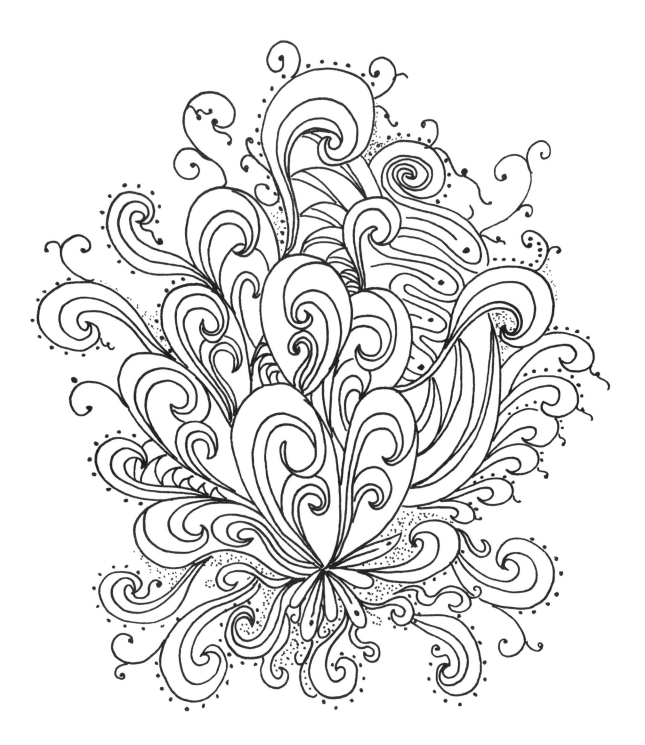

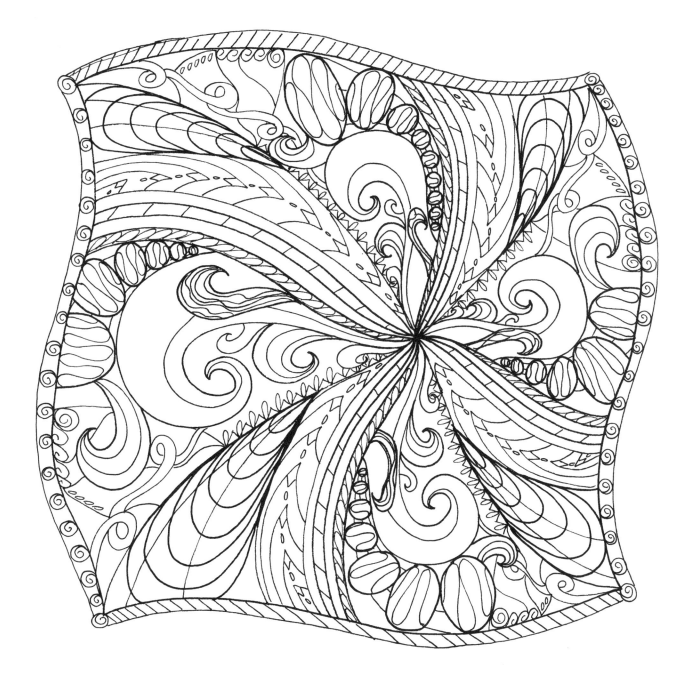

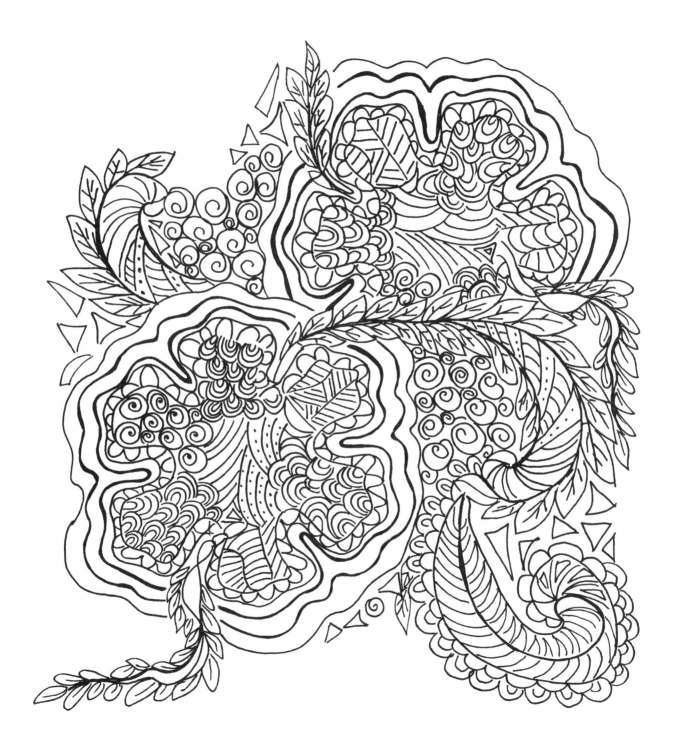

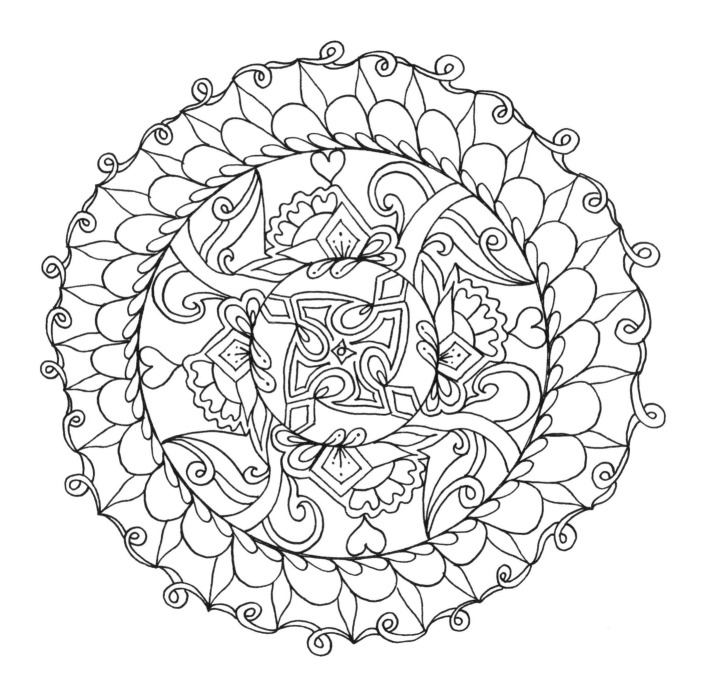

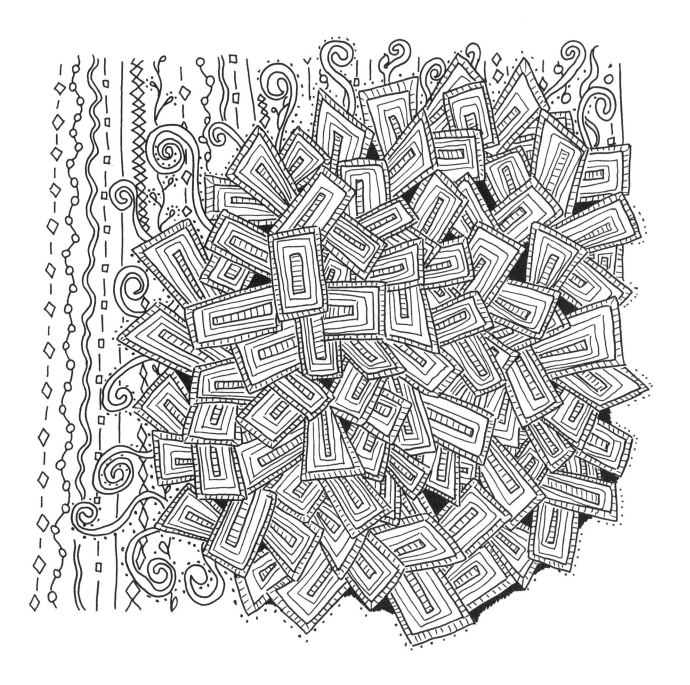

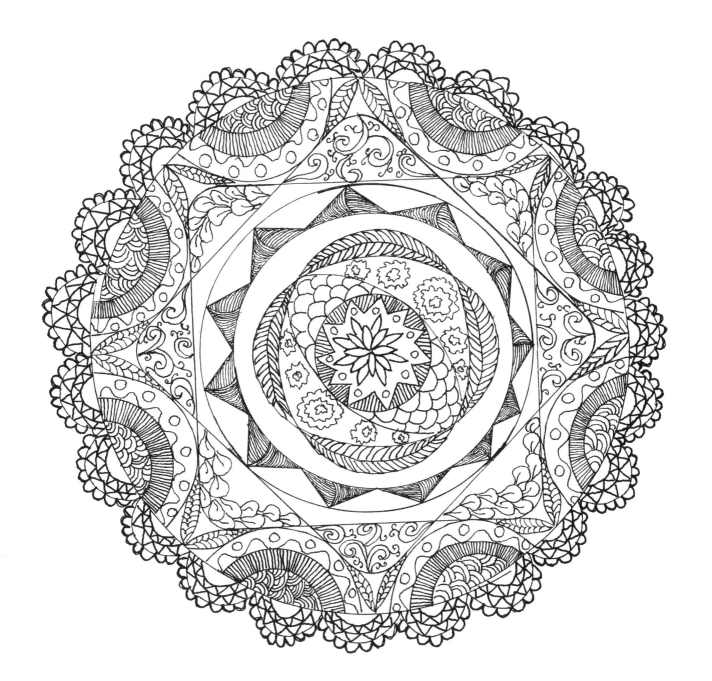

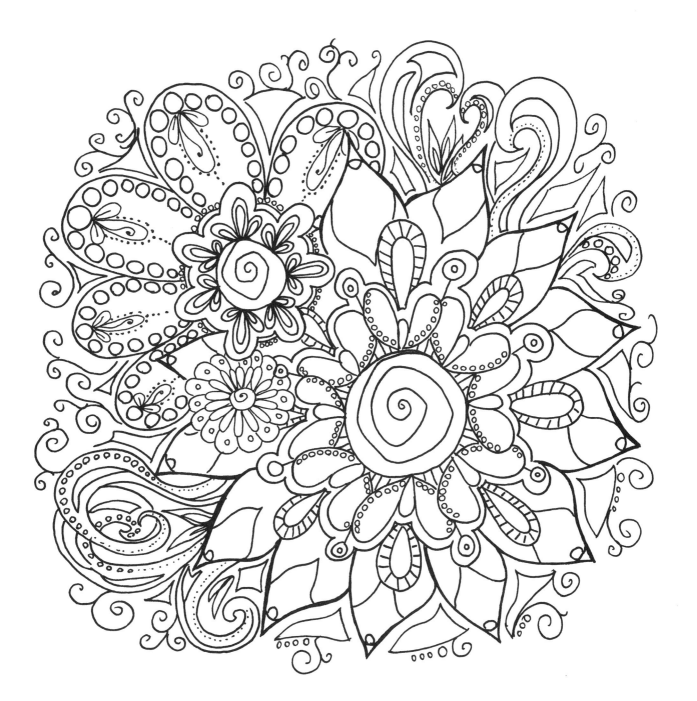

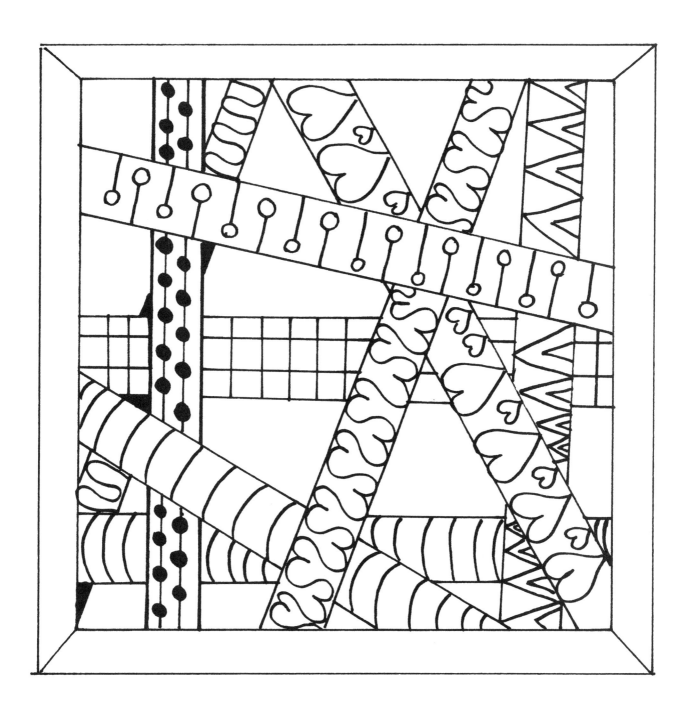

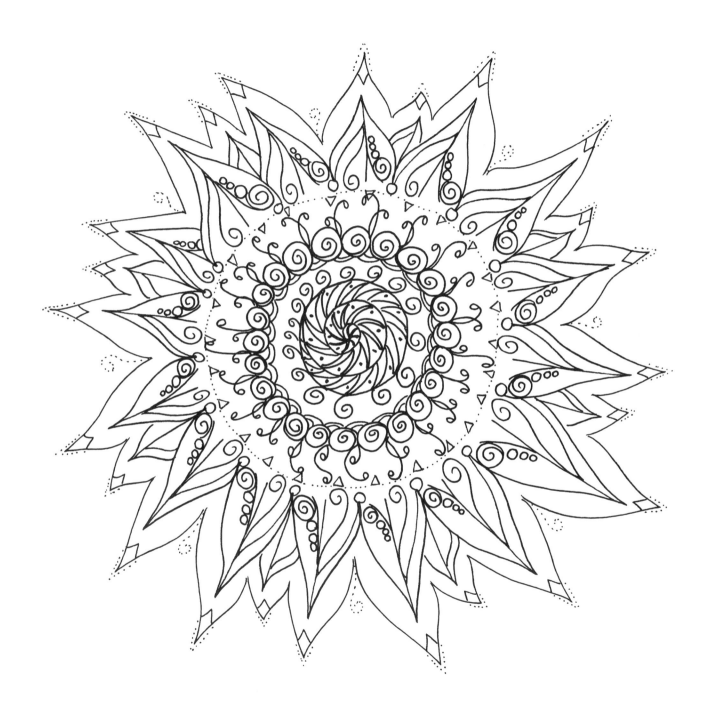

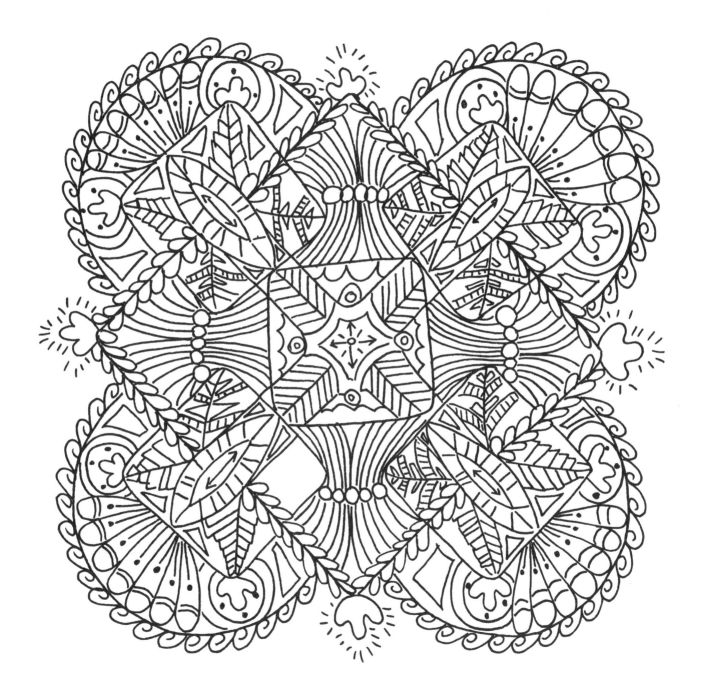

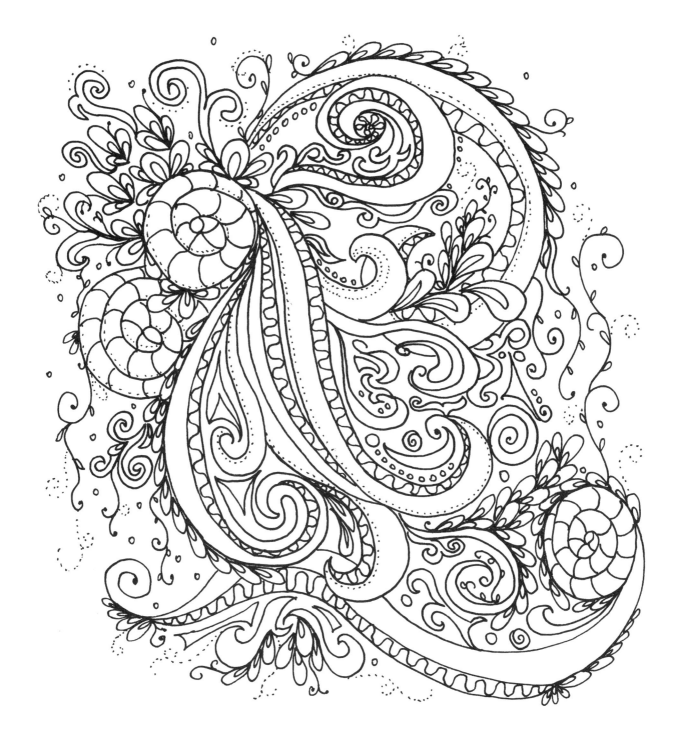

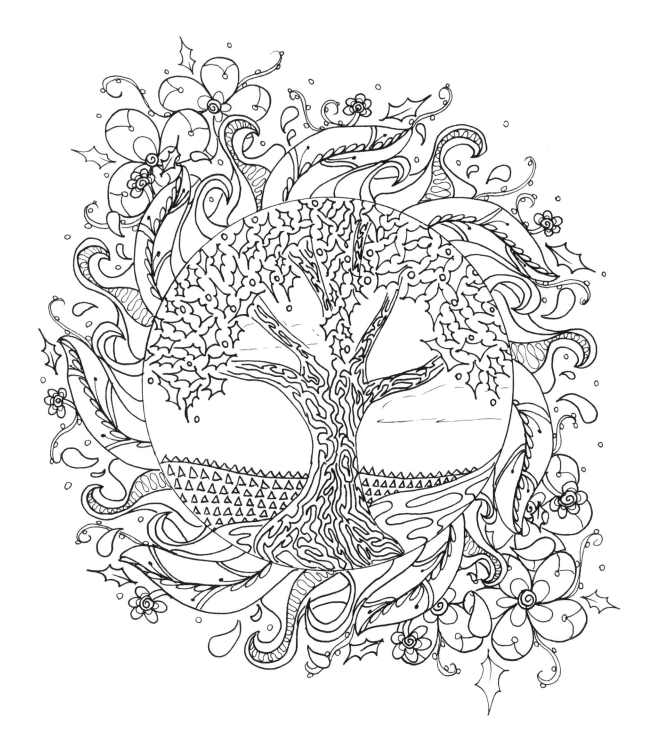

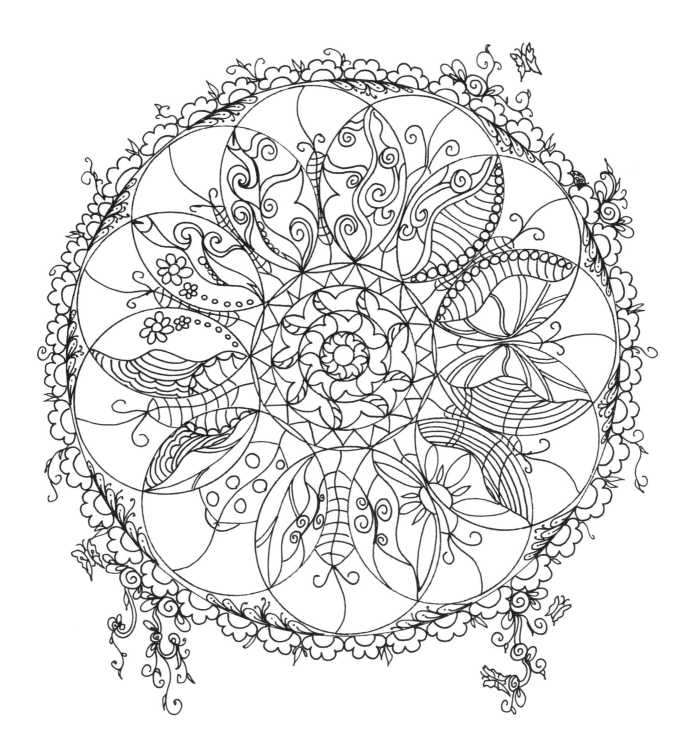

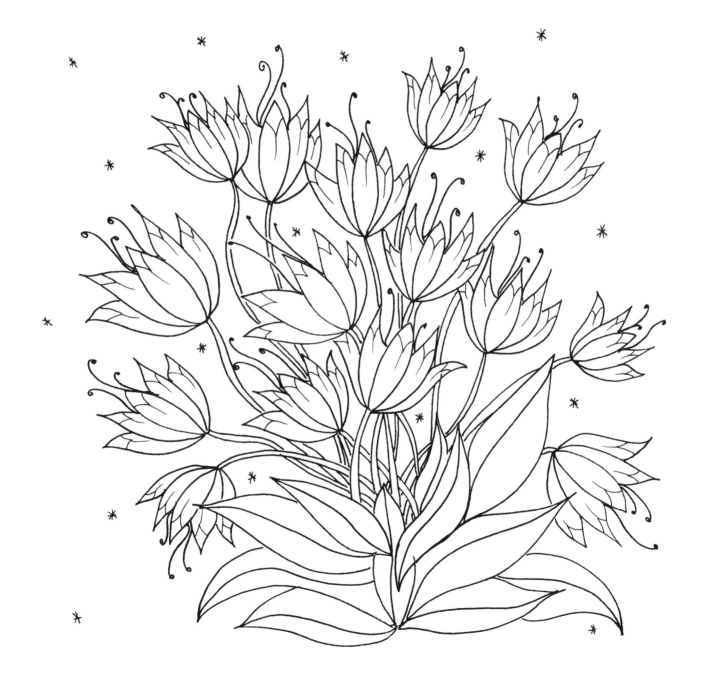

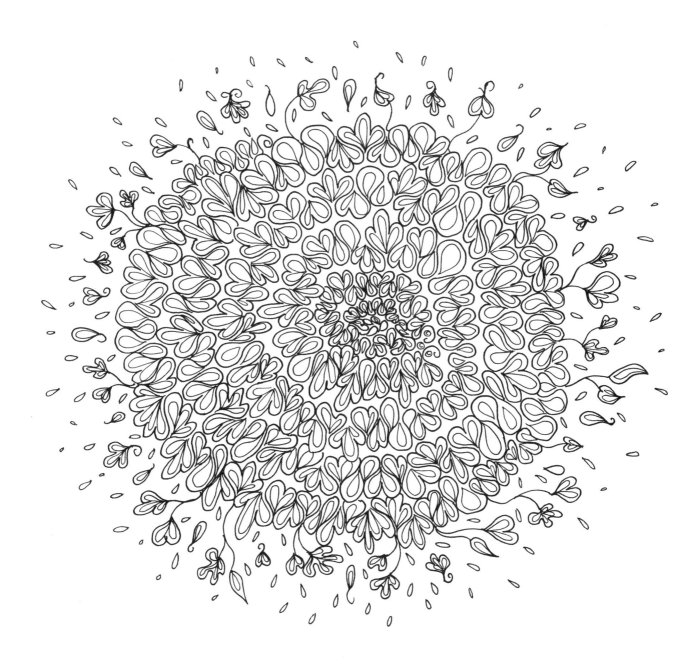

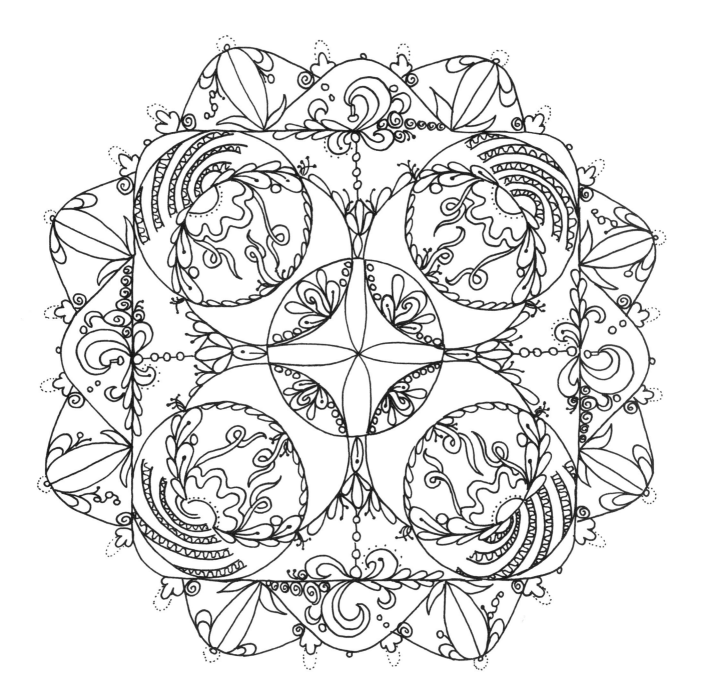

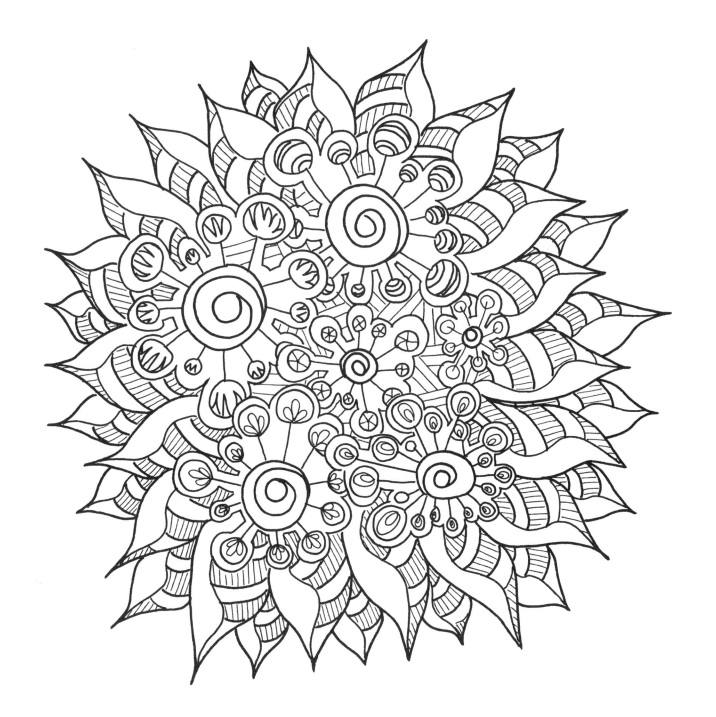

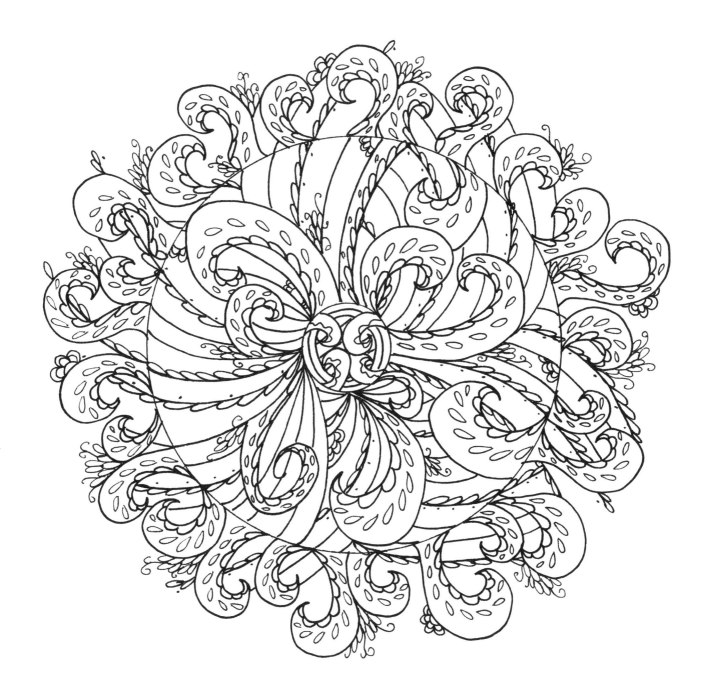

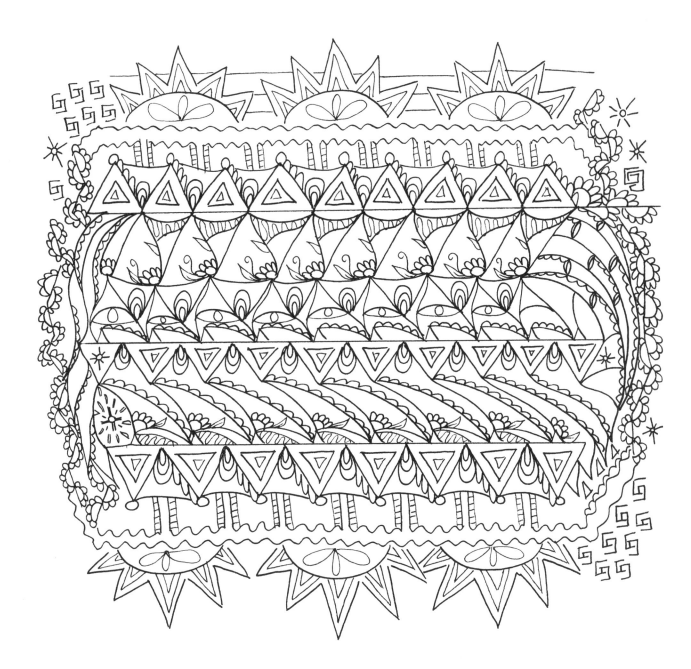

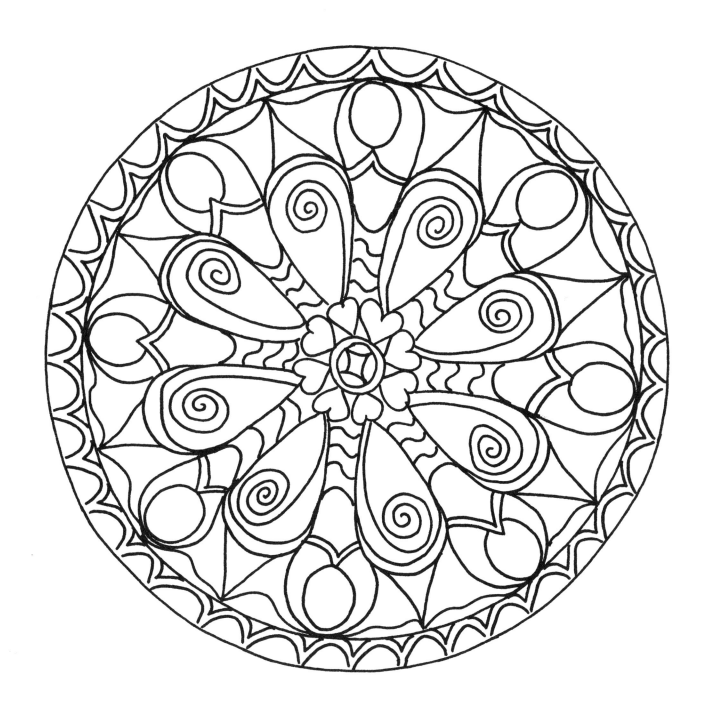

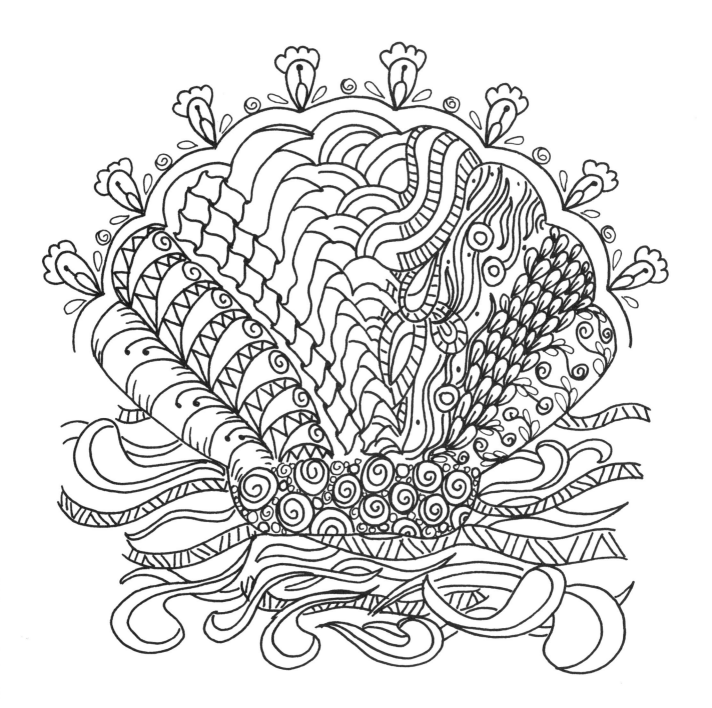

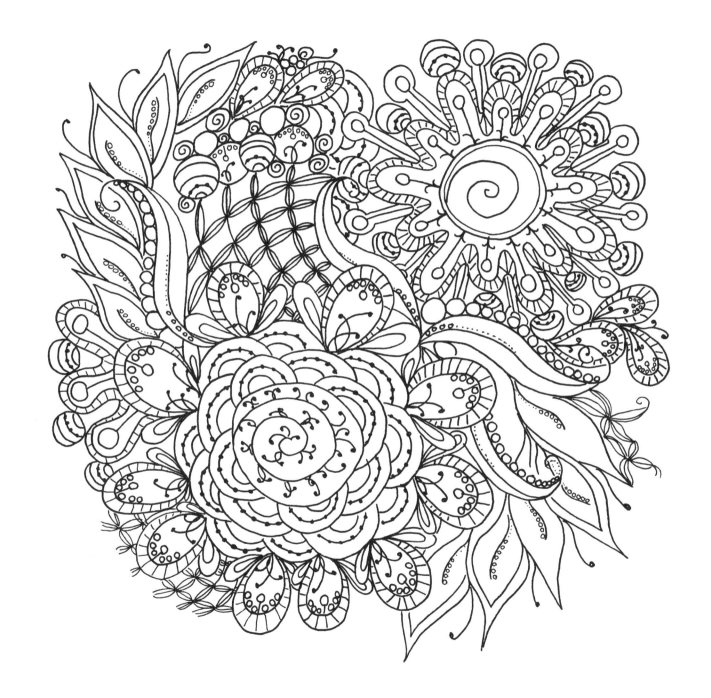

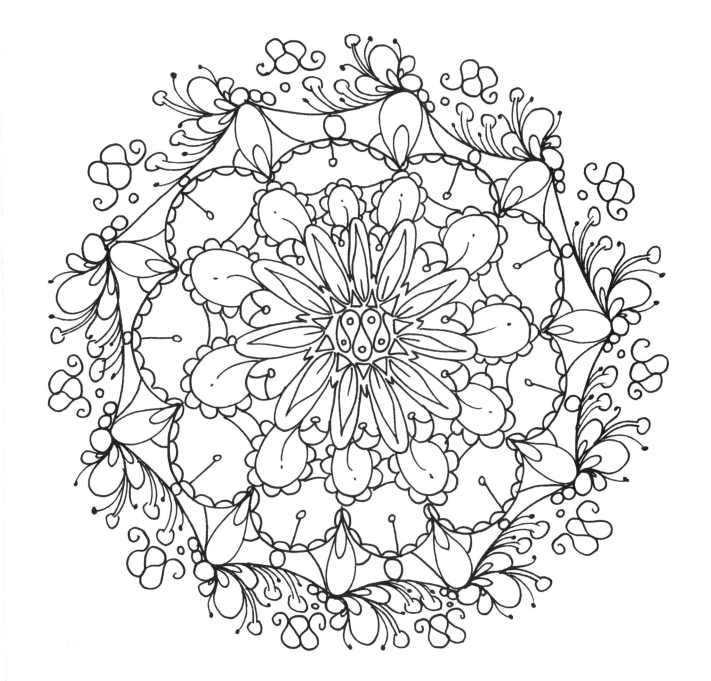

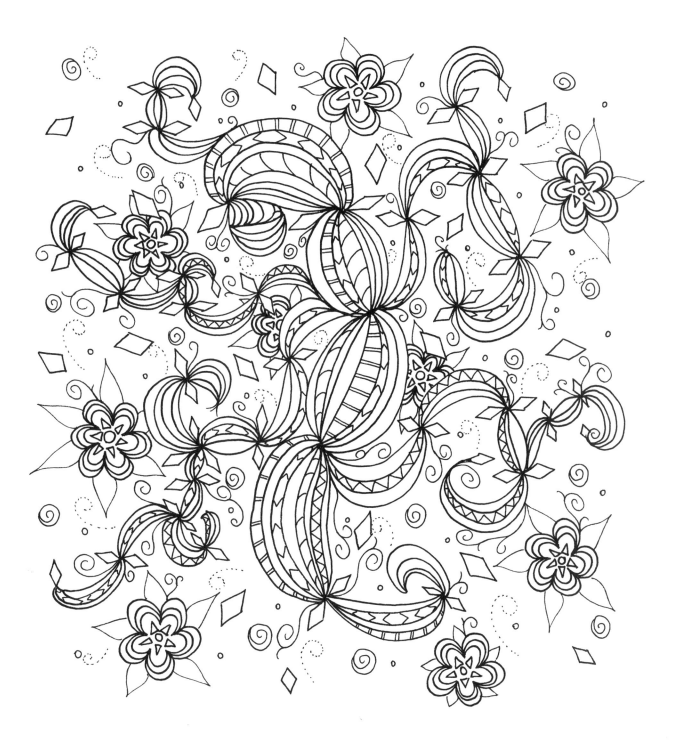

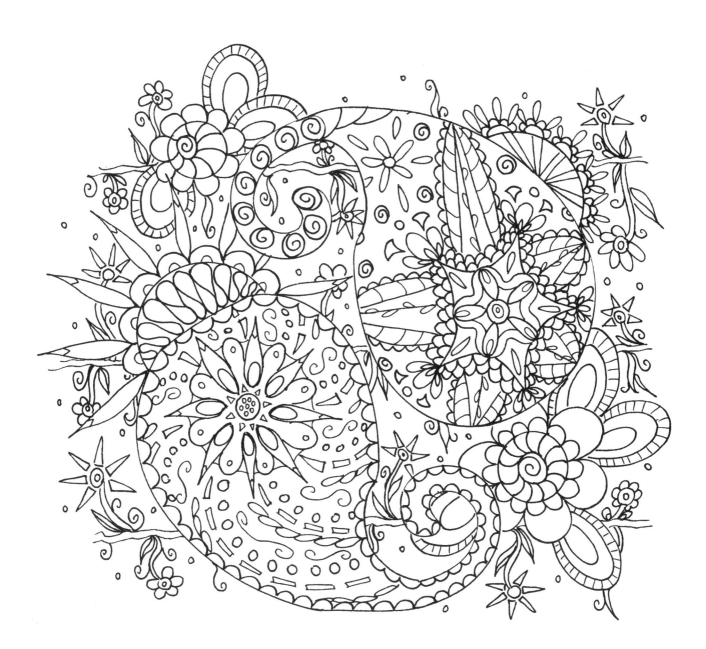

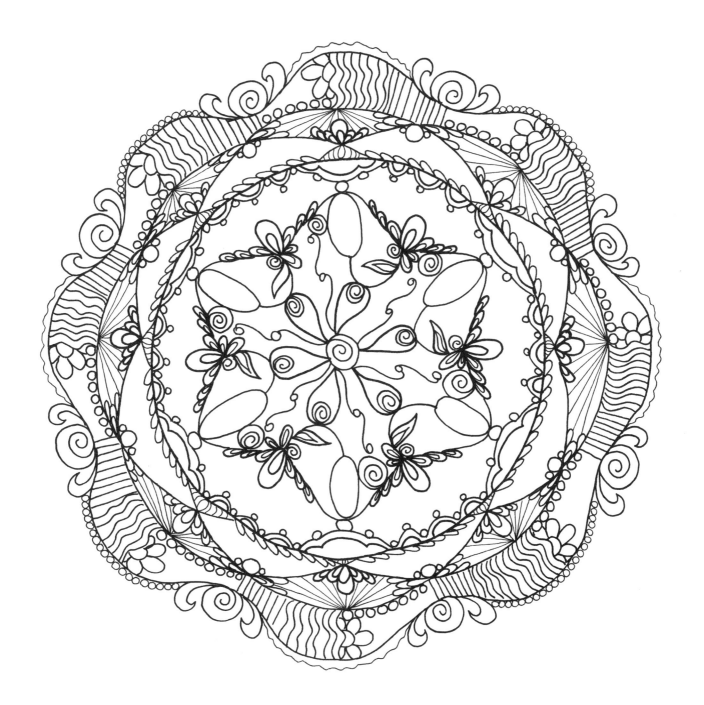

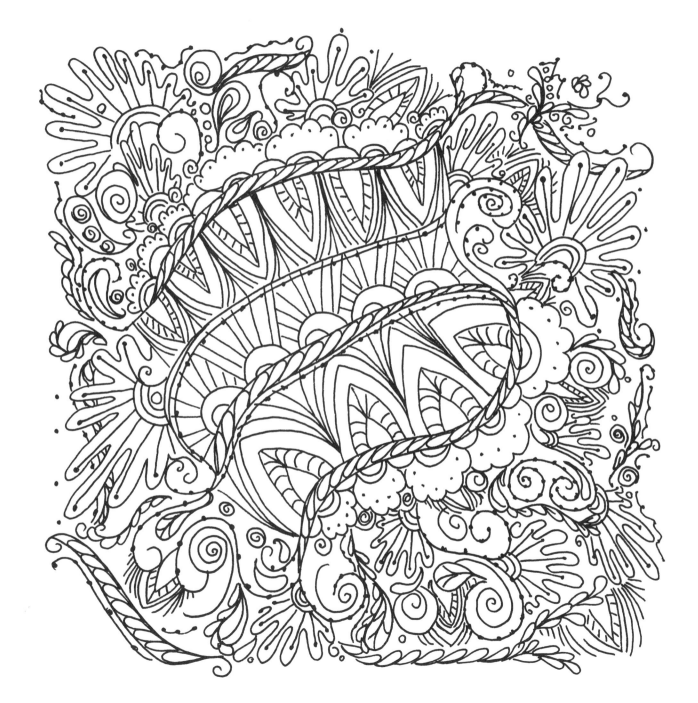

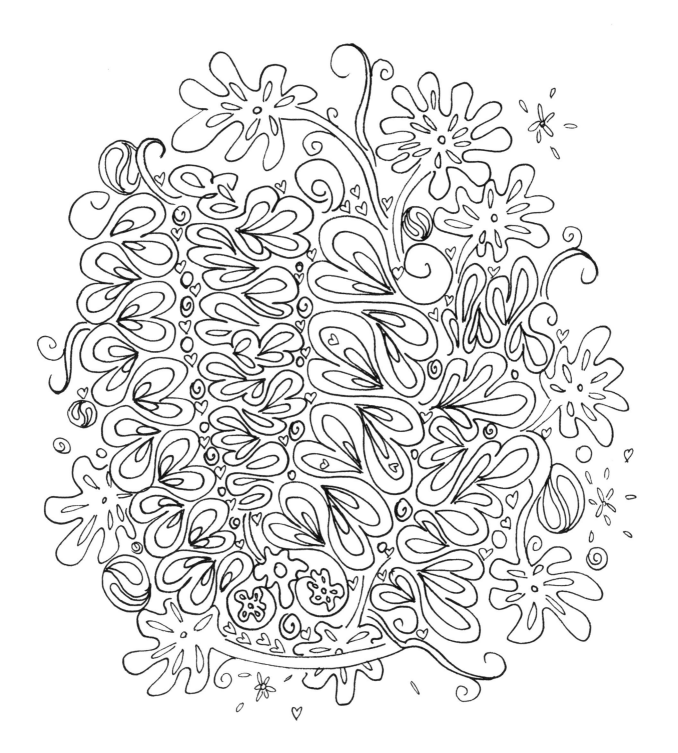

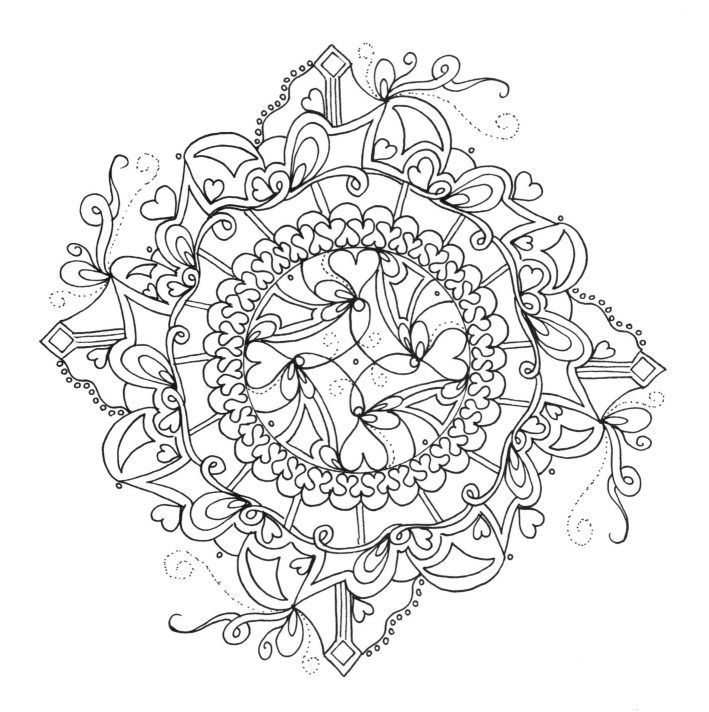

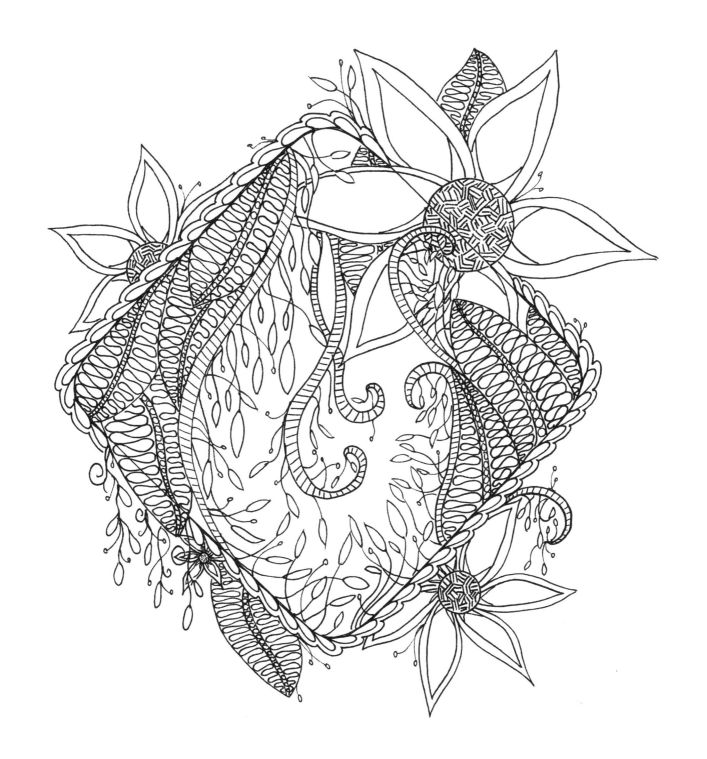

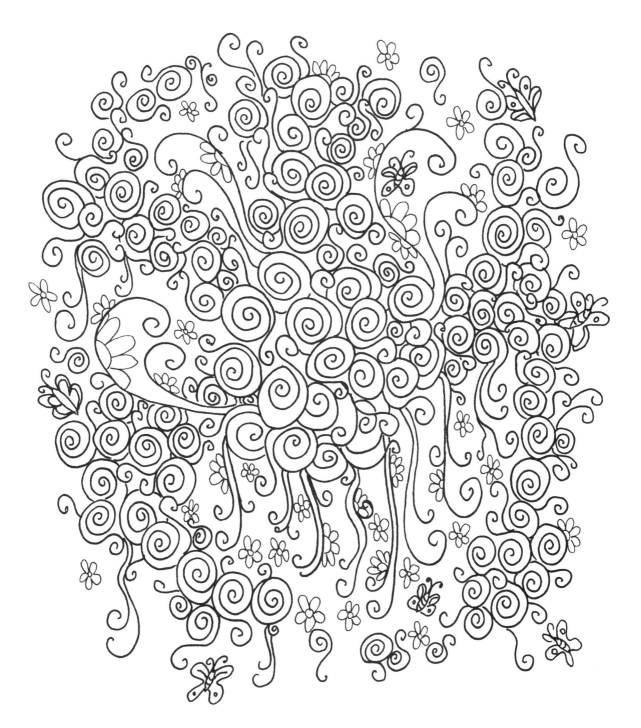

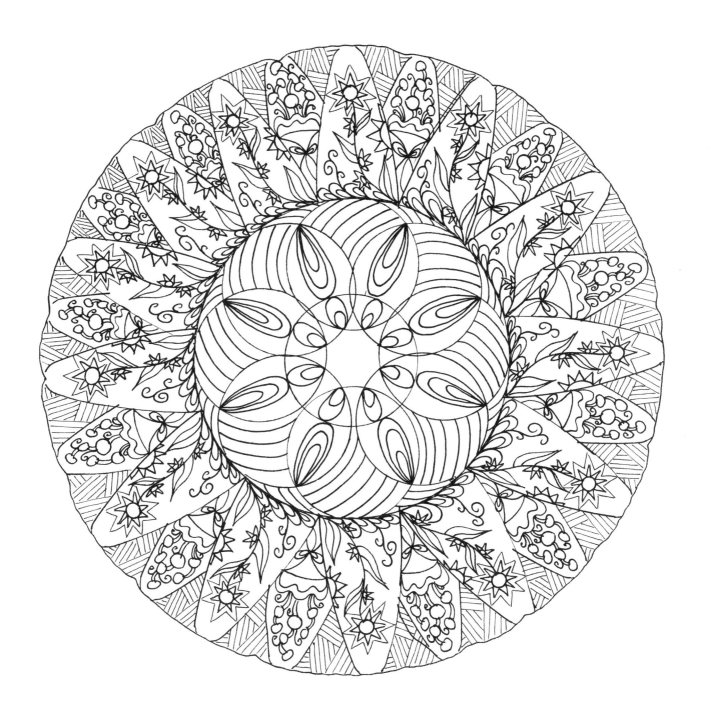

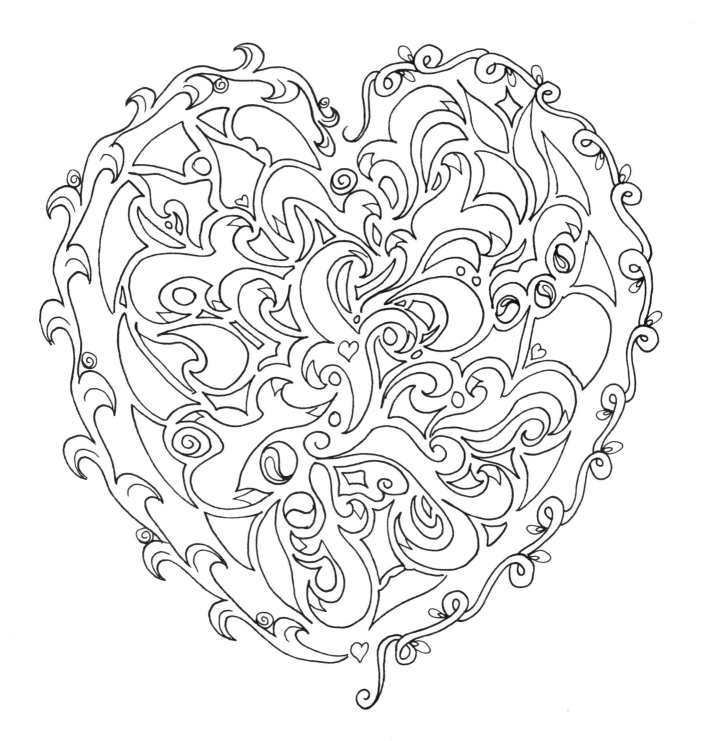

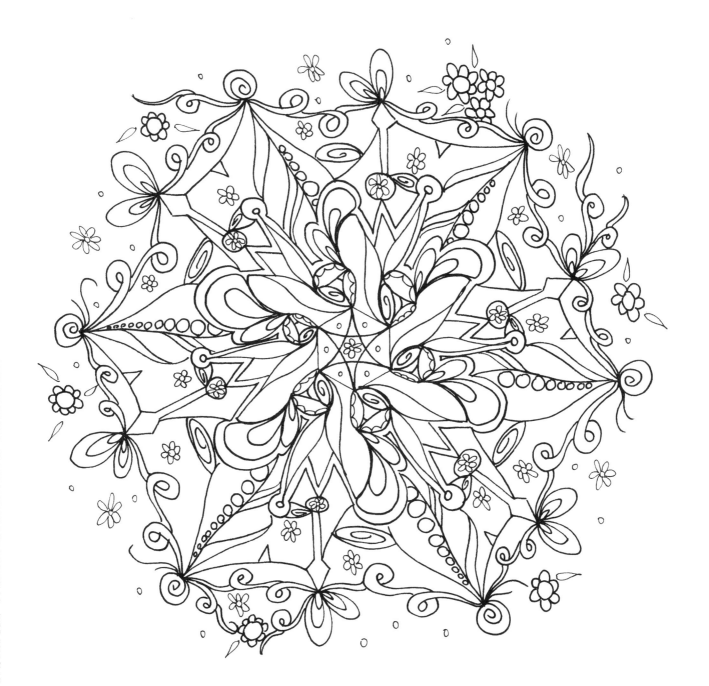

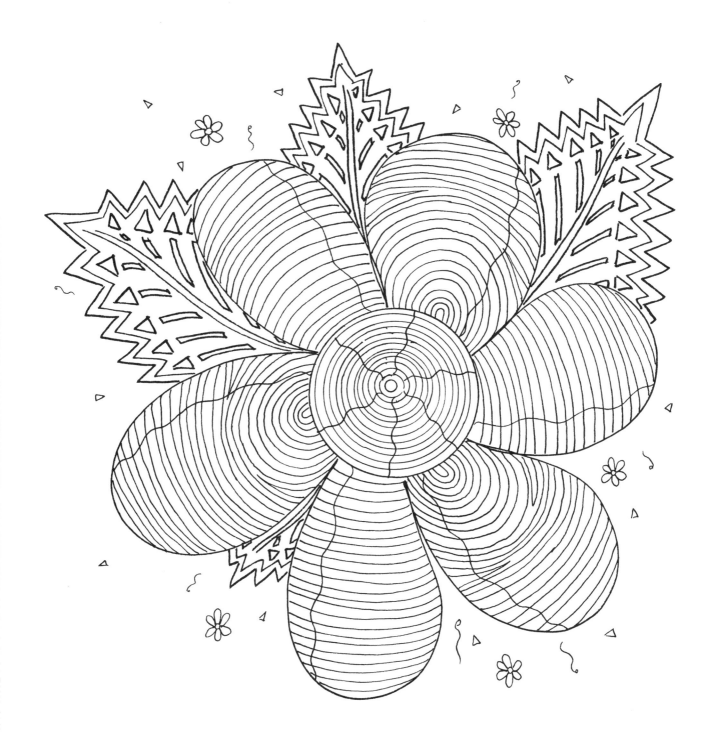

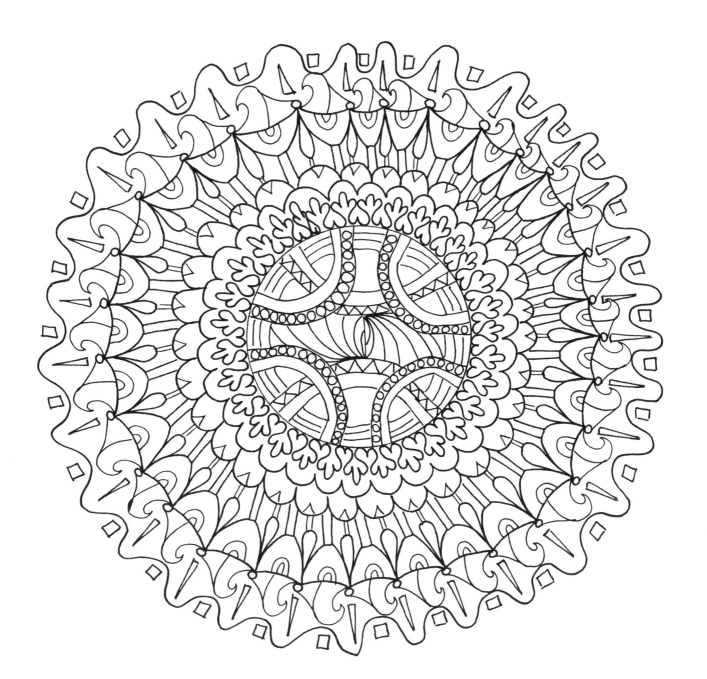

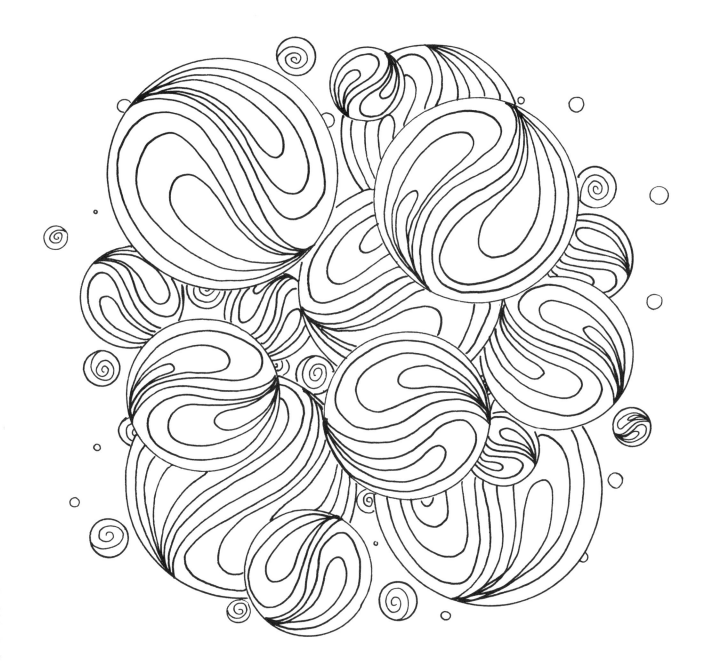

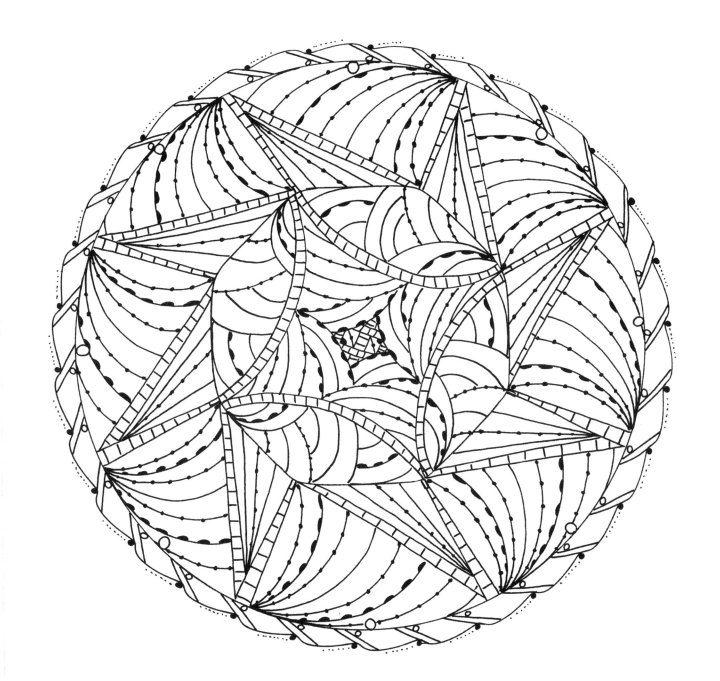

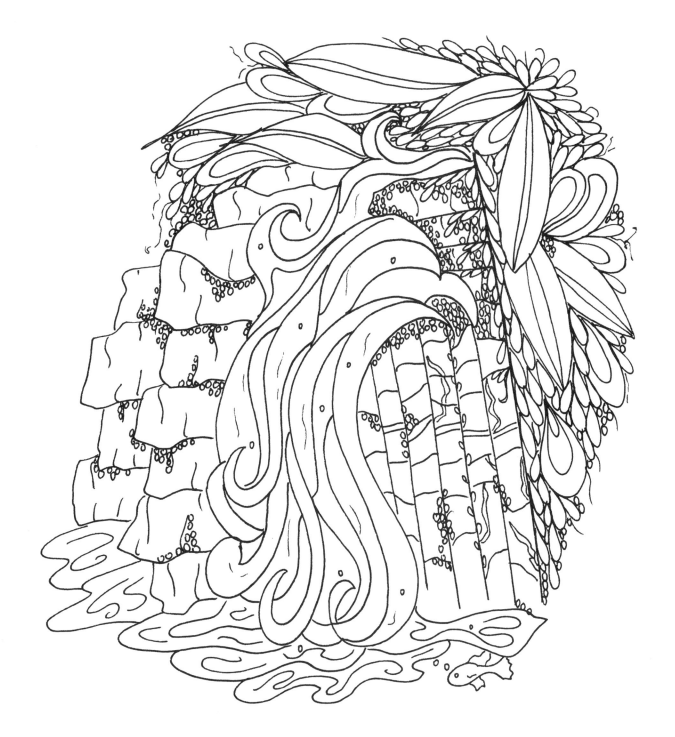

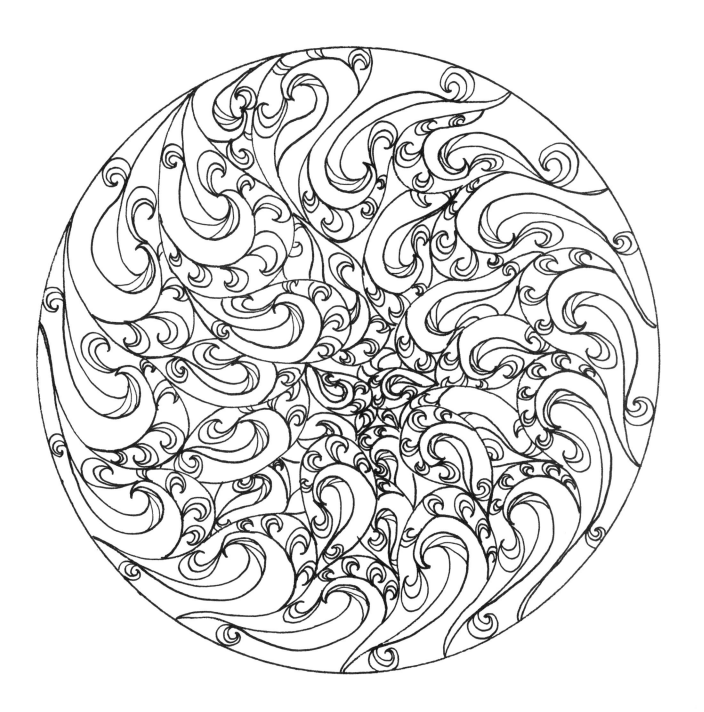

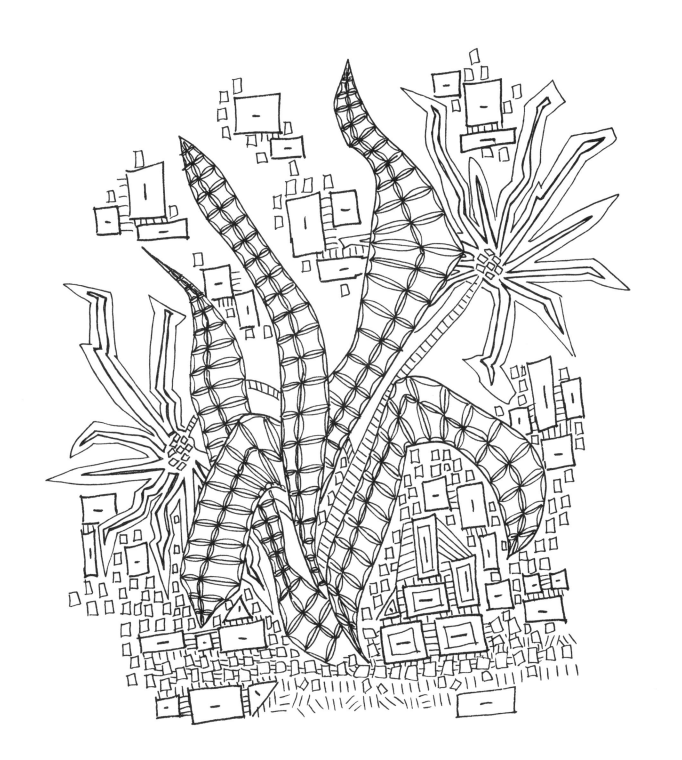

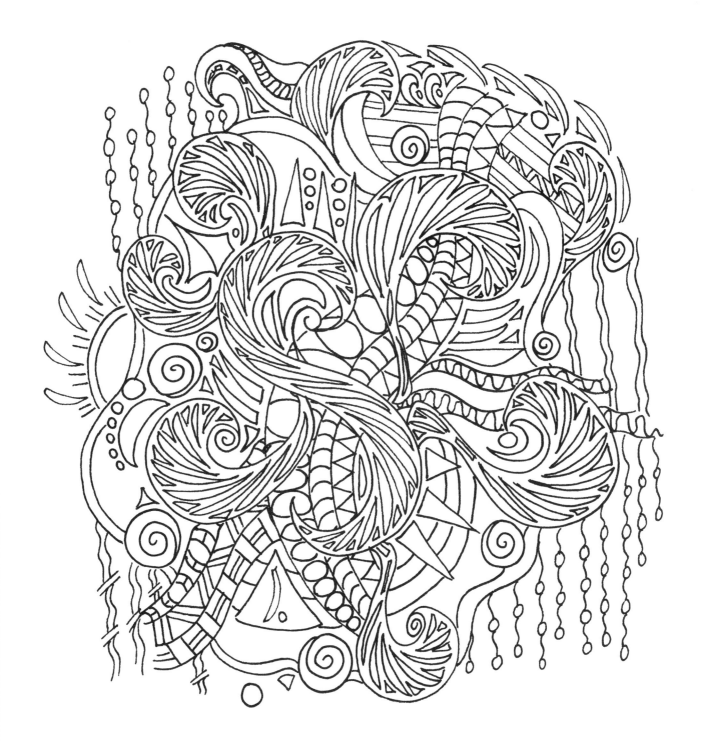

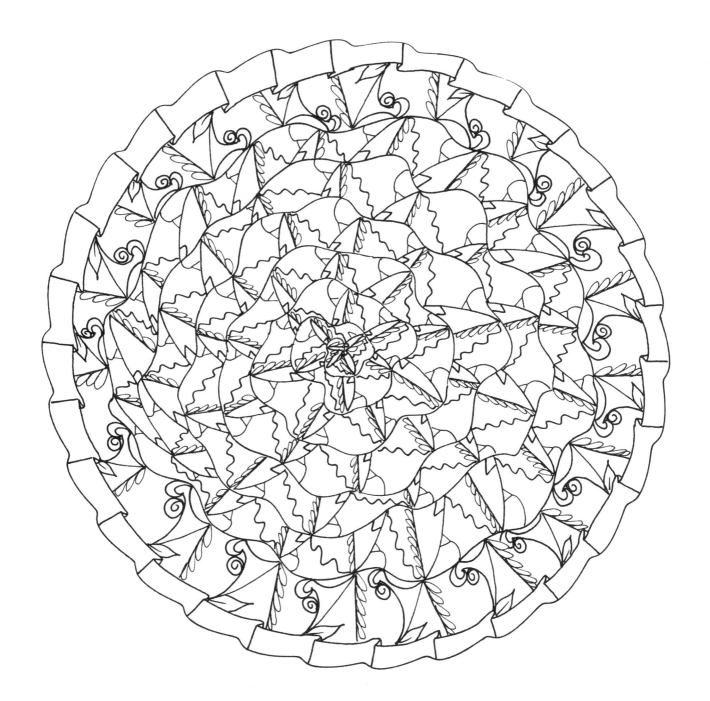

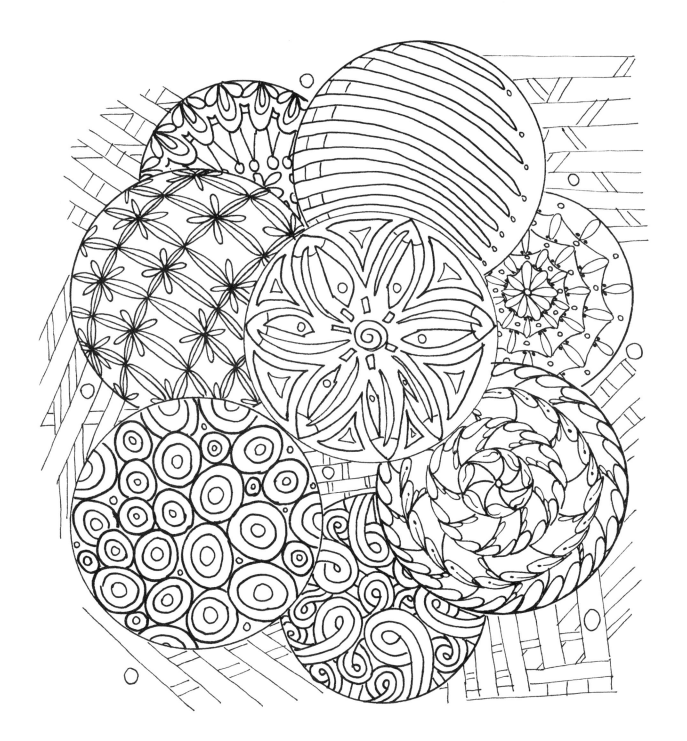

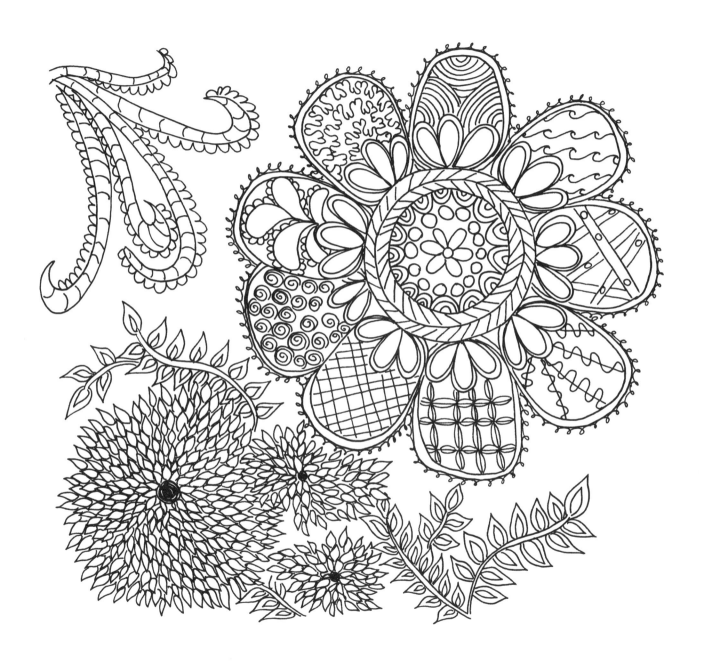

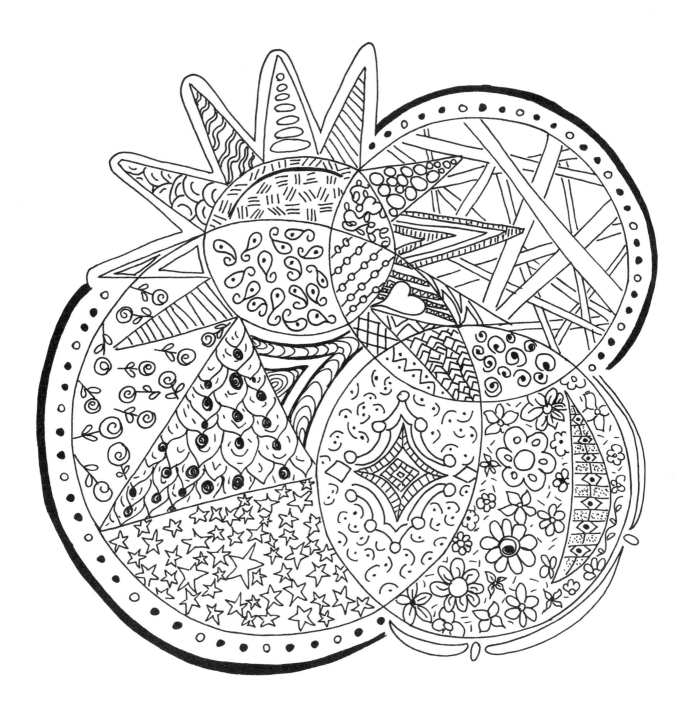

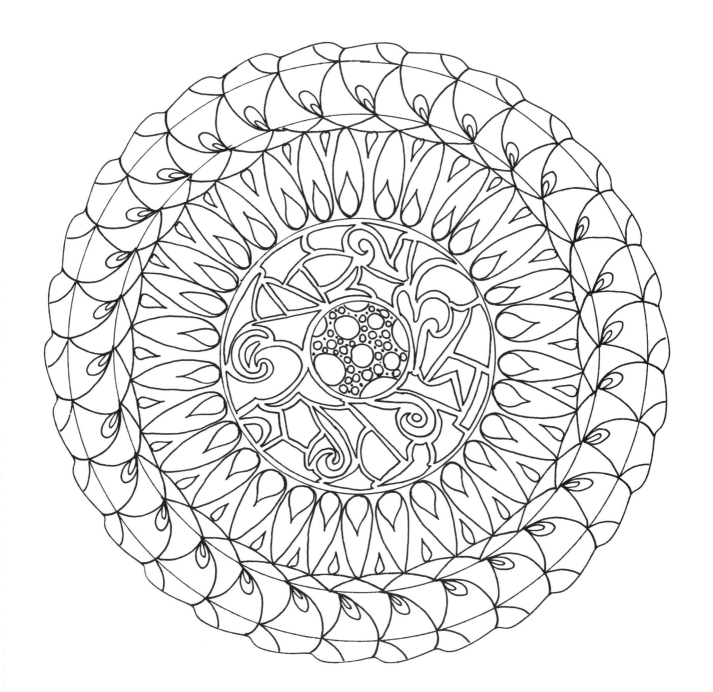

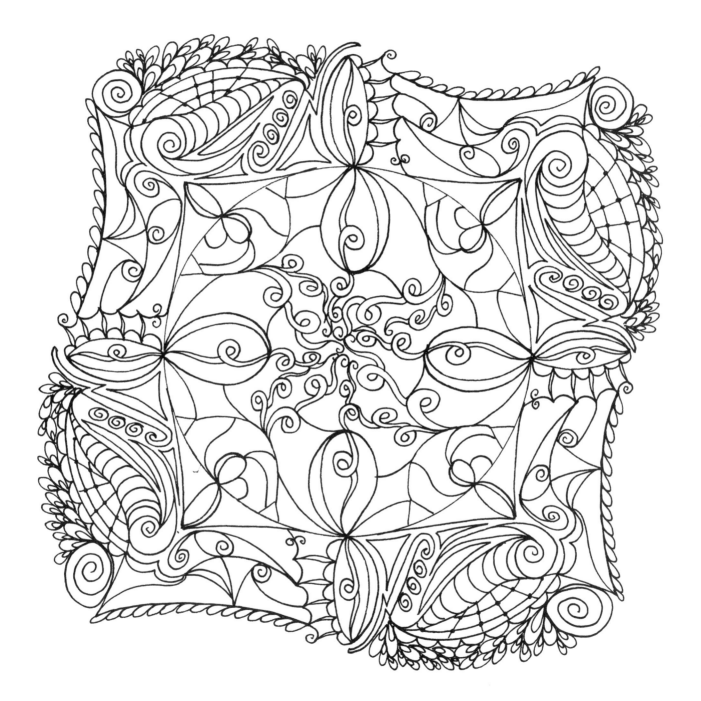

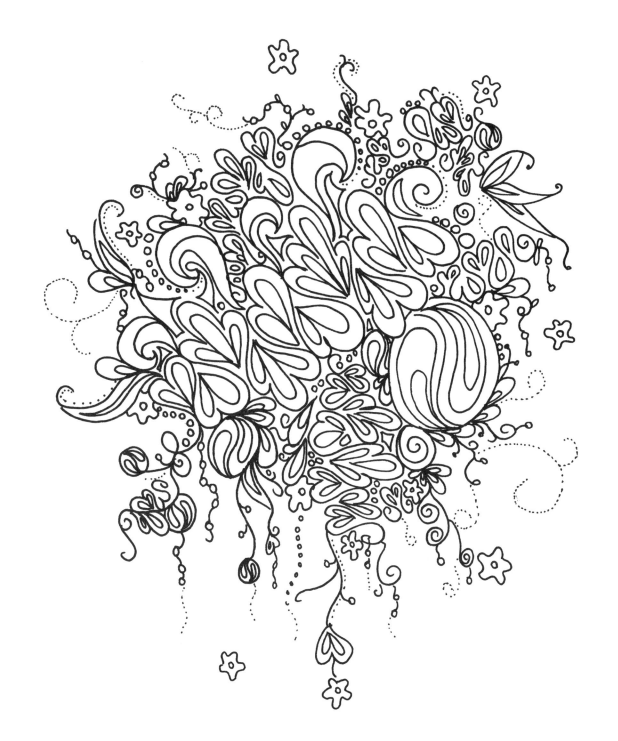

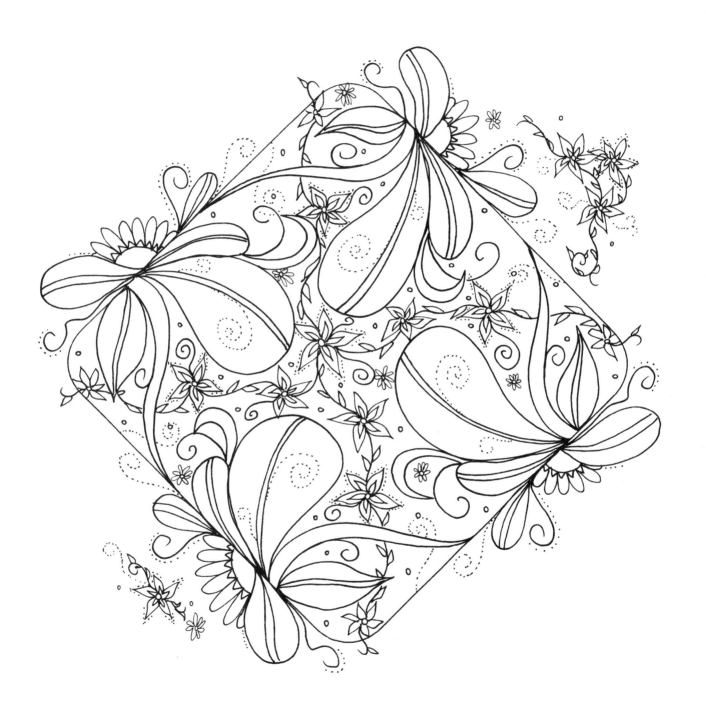